D0849357

W. SOMERSET MAUGHAM
and his world

FREDERIC RAPHAEL

W. SOMERSET MAUGHAM
and his world

CHAMPLAIN COLLEGE

with 110 illustrations

THAMES AND HUDSON

LONDON

Frontispiece, Somerset Maugham in his
later years; a characteristic portrait by the
London photographer Baron.

Printed by Jarrold and Sons Ltd, Norwich

WILLIAM SOMERSET MAUGHAM was born on 25 January 1874 at the British
Embassy in Paris. His father, Robert Ormond Maugham, was solicitor to the
Embassy; he and his wife, Edith Mary, *née* Snell, already had three sons. William
was to be their last. They lived in the avenue d'Antin, but Mrs Maugham gave birth
to her child within the precincts of the Embassy so that he might enjoy the privilege of
being born on British soil. In 1874 there was no soil quite like it.

Mrs Maugham was very small and very beautiful. She had large brown eyes and
her hair was of a rich, reddish gold. She is said to have had exquisite features and
lovely skin. Her husband was very ugly. Yet he was a man of lively mind and
temperament. He travelled widely, in Morocco, Greece, Turkey and Asia Minor.
He collected books and souvenirs, among them an Algerian device said to be a
specific against the evil eye. He was twenty years older than the wife whose beauty
enabled her to move confidently in Parisian society and to invite fashionable people to
her tea-parties. When William was born it was but four years since the Commune
had threatened to take Paris out of the hands of the great, but the great had returned
and their hands were firmly on the reins of power. The Prussians had returned across
the Rhine, taking Alsace and Lorraine with them, so to speak, but Paris had
recovered, like a beautiful woman after a rape, and who now spoke of those terrible
days? The pursuit of love was once again more important than the pursuit of revenge
or of social justice. Someone once asked the beautiful Mrs Maugham why she
continued to be faithful to that ugly little man, her husband. She replied that he had
never hurt her feelings. They were known in Paris as Beauty and the Beast.

Both of William's parents belonged to middle-class families. His mother's father,
a Major in the Indian Army, died soon after her birth, in Trichinopoly. Edith's sister,

The British Embassy in Paris, where
Somerset Maugham was born.

Somerset Maugham's mother; this photograph was always beside his bed at the Villa Mauresque, Cap Ferrat.

Robert Maugham, Somerset's father.

Rose Ellen, was born after her father's death and the young widow took her two daughters to France, where she made a living by writing novels and children's books in French. In 1863 Edith married Robert Ormond Maugham; she was twenty-three. The ceremony, like William's birth, took place in the British Embassy.

The Maughams were slightly grander than the Snells or the Todds, Edith's mother's family, though the latter boasted a connection with General Sir Henry Somerset (1794–1862), the godfather of Mrs Maugham's uncle, Henry Somerset Todd, from whom derived the unusual name which William was to parade in public all his life and by which none of his friends, if they were wise, would ever call him. Robert Ormond Maugham's father, Robert, was also a solicitor. He came from a relatively humble family (his own father was a clerk who barely made a living in Regency London), but he was as diligent as he was commonplace and he became sufficiently successful and respected to be appointed, at a meeting in Furnival's Inn in June 1825, secretary and solicitor of The Law Institution. This body, now known as 'The Law Society', built itself impressive premises in Chancery Lane and, with Robert Maugham largely in charge (he had an apartment on the premises and a salary of £400 a year, for part-time services), grew to be as important in the profession and training of solicitors as the Inns of Court have always been in the life of the Bar. Robert Maugham also had time to continue the editorship of the *Legal Observer*, which he had founded in 1830, an act of enterprise which entitles him to be called 'the Father of Legal Journalism'. He was not always quite the model of decorum, at least in his private habits, which the severe standards of the Institution might have required of a candidate in its examinations. His grandson, in *The Summing Up*, rehearses the evidence of an articled clerk, Albert Dixon, who was invited to dinner in the apartment in Chancery Lane:

My grandfather carved the beef, and then a servant handed a dish of potatoes baked in their skins. There are few things better to eat than a potato in its skin, with plenty of butter, pepper and salt, but apparently my grandfather did not think so. He rose in his chair at the head of the table and took the potatoes out of the dish one by one and threw them at each picture on the walls. Then without a word he sat down again and went on with his dinner.

Robert Maugham had six children. Three were daughters. Of the sons, one, Frederick, was drowned when the steamship *Prince*, on which he had volunteered to serve as a purser, went down in the Black Sea on 14 November 1854, half a mile out from Balaclava Harbour, with the loss of 144 men; the second, Henry MacDonald, went into the Church of England; and the third, Robert Ormond, married the lovely Edith whose photograph William Somerset Maugham was to keep by his bedside for the whole of his long, long life.

William had three brothers, but he could hardly be said to have been brought up with them. By the time he was four, they were all at a minor public school, Dover College, in England. William had the illusion of being an only child, like Philip in his autobiographical novel, *Of Human Bondage*. He shared a room with his French nurse, but often he was able to spend a little time alone with his mother in her bedroom in the mornings, and in the afternoons he was (unusually for the period)

The Paris of Somerset Maugham's childhood; a painting of the Place du Carrousel in the late nineteenth century by Vicenta de Paredes.

The Avenue des Champs-Elysées towards
the turn of the century.

welcome in the *salon* where men like Clemenceau, then leader of the extreme Left in
the Chamber of Deputies, would come to take *thé à l'anglaise*. Sometimes they would
listen to the small boy recite the La Fontaine fable that was his party-piece. He learned
early to sing for his supper. At other times he went with his nurse and played with
other children of the right kind in the Champs-Elysées. One of them, Violet
Hammersley, *née* Williams-Freeman, also born in the British Embassy and Edith
Maugham's god-daughter, recalled him vividly:

. . . he told us wonderful stories. And he was highly imaginative. When my mother
was 'at home' on Sunday afternoons, we children were also allowed to invite our
friends to tea. Willie often came, and because he was so imaginative he was allowed
to invent the games we should play.

Willie also joined us sometimes in the Champs-Elysées, which was a great
meeting place for children. We formed ourselves into clans to play such games as *Les
Barres* and *La Tour prend garde*. Willie used to fascinate us by passing off imitation sous
at the kiosques where paper windmills and coloured balloons were sold together with
pieces of flat gingerbread pricked out in patterns. And he passed off his false sous to
the itinerant old woman who had a tin strapped to her from which she used to sell
gaufrettes powdered with icing sugar. My elder sister was very shocked by Willie's
trickery, but my youngest brother and I thought it was very clever that these fierce-
looking traders could be gulled by this innocent-looking boy.

Mrs Maugham's life was one of sober elegance and of modest privilege which her
husband had to work hard to maintain. But Edith was a sick woman and often in

pain. She suffered from tuberculosis, for which no better cure could then be offered than the gentle air of a resort like Pau, under the lee of the Pyrenees, to which they escaped from the harsh winter climate of the capital. There were also trips to the seaside. On the beach at Trouville the little boy watched an artist trying to sell his work to the buttoned crowd. A Boudin at five francs was not excessively priced, but not many seemed inclined to buy. Eighty years later, Maugham was to see one of those little pictures (infinite beach in tiny frame) in the window of a New York gallery. The price was $7,000.

In late 1881, Edith Maugham realized that she had not long to live. One day, far gone in yet another pregnancy (it was imagined that childbearing was sovereign against tuberculosis), she struggled from her bed, dressed herself in a white satin evening gown and went to a photographer's. When she returned, she collapsed. In January 1882, she died in childbed. She was forty-one. William was eight years old on the 25th of the same month. He never ceased to adore her. Even as an old man he would say, 'I shall never get over her death. I shall never get over it.'

The tragedy was compounded by the death of his father only two years later. The ugly little man had just finished building a summer house at Suresnes, outside Paris, a house on a hill, with green shutters, which no Maugham was to occupy. He died 'of cancer and grief', and perhaps overwork, on the eve of his son's tenth birthday. Maugham said later that his father was a stranger to him, but he was a stranger who seemed both rich and protective. The small boy, who had lived a life of cosseted indulgence with two parents who cared much for each other, was an orphan. His brothers were too old and too busy to be of comfort. Frederick, the nearest in age, was

The beach at Trouville.

at Cambridge, where he was having a brilliant academic and sporting success. What was to be done with the boy? He spoke little English (evidence of how thoroughly at home in France the family was) and he had hurriedly to be coached in the language – a crash course indeed – by an English clergyman who was attached to the Embassy. The method chosen was mainly that of reading aloud from police-court reports in *The Standard*, including that of a terrifying murder in a train between Paris and Calais.

Accompanied by his nurse, he was soon shipped to England, the native land whose language he could hardly speak. He told later of standing on the quayside at Dover and calling, 'Porteur! Cabriolet!' The French influence on his character and style can scarcely be overemphasized. French locutions always haunted his prose and French literature was to be closer to his heart than the English to which he was so cruelly transported. The child's destination was Whitstable, in Kent, a gloomy little port, famous for its oysters. (They were a shilling a dozen in 1884.) There he was wished upon his uncle, the stiff and childless Henry MacDonald, and his wife, a German-born lady called Barbara Sophia, *née* von Scheidlin. The nurse who had brought him and who had been his mother's maid, the only link between the boy and the lost paradise of his Parisian childhood, was sent away the next day. He found himself a stranger in a strange land, at the chilly mercy of a cowed *Hausfrau* and her snobbish, joyless husband, a childless couple no happier to see him than he was to see them.

He was sent to a preparatory school at Canterbury. If the rectory at Whitstable was as cold as charity (one of the clichés of which Maugham was often to avail himself in later years), there was little warmth at the annexe to the King's School. He encountered the practised cruelty of the English schoolboy. The stammer which had passed unremarked in Paris was now the butt of all the bruising xenophobia of the sons of an Empire at its zenith.

He remembered the arrogance of the British of the eighties all his life:

> Great Britain was at the height of her power. A map showed in pink vast stretches of the earth's surface under the sovereignty of Queen Victoria. The mother country was immensely rich. The British were the world's bankers. British commerce sent its products to the uttermost parts of the earth, and their quality was generally acknowledged to be higher than those manufactured by any other nation. Peace reigned except for small punitive expeditions here and there. The army, though small, was confident (notwithstanding the reverse on Majuba Hill) that it could hold its own against any force that was likely to be brought against it. The British navy was

BOVRIL
NOUGHT SHALL MAKE US RUE, IF ENGLAND TO ITSELF DO REST BUT TRUE AND TAKES
Beecham's Pills.
WORTH A GUINEA A BOX

Advertising in the service of British superiority.

W w
W w
W is the Word
Of an Englishman true:
When given, it means
What he says, he will do.
W. w.

The self-esteem of the British in the 1880s; page from a children's book called *ABC for Baby Patriots*

British sightseers in the Canary Islands, 1905.

the greatest in the world. In sport the British were supreme. None could compete with them in the games they played, and in the classic races it was almost unheard-of that a horse from abroad should win. It looked as though nothing could ever change this happy state of things. The inhabitants of these islands of ours trusted in God, and God, they were assured, had taken the British Empire under his particular protection. It is true that the Irish were making a nuisance of themselves. It is true that the factory workers were underpaid and overworked. But that seemed an inevitable consequence of the industrialisation of the country and there was nothing to do about it. The reformers who tried to improve their lot were regarded as mischievous troublemakers. It is true that the agricultural labourers lived in miserable hovels and earned a pitiful wage, but the Ladies Bountiful of the landowners were kind to them. Many of them occupied themselves with their moral welfare, sent them beef tea and calves-foot jelly when they were ill and often clothes for their children. People said there always had been rich and poor in the world and always would be, and that seemed to settle the matter.

The British travelled a great deal on the Continent. They crowded the health resorts, Spa, Vichy, Homburg, Aix-les-Bains and Baden-Baden. In winter they went to the Riviera. They built themselves sumptuous villas at Cannes and Monte Carlo. Vast hotels were erected to accommodate them. They had plenty of money and they spent it freely. They felt that they were a race apart and no sooner had they landed at Calais than it was borne in upon them that they were now among natives, not of course natives as were the Indians or the Chinese, but – natives. They alone washed, and the baths that they frequently travelled with were a tangible proof that they were not as others. They were healthy, athletic, sensible, and in every way superior. Because they enjoyed their sojourn among the natives whose habits were so curiously un-English, because, though they thought them frivolous (the French), lazy (the Italians), stupid but funny (the Germans), with the kindness of heart natural to them, they liked them. It never entered their heads that the courtesy which they received, the bows, the smiles, the desire to please were owing to their lavish spending, and that behind their backs the 'natives' mocked them for their uncouth dress, their gawkiness, their bad manners, their insolence, their silliness in letting themselves be consistently overcharged, their patronizing tolerance; and it required disastrous wars for it to dawn upon them how greatly they had been mistaken.

Somerset Maugham as a boy with his
uncle, the Reverend Henry MacDonald
Maugham, the Rector of Whitstable,
about 1885.

The High Street, Whitstable; a
photograph about 1890.

Opposite, Somerset Maugham as a
schoolboy in England.

The forbidding entrance to King's School, Canterbury. 'The high brick wall in front of the school gave it the look of a prison' (*Of Human Bondage*).

So bad did his stammer now become that one day, sent home alone from London by his uncle, who intended to stay the night in town, he was unable to name his destination at the ticket-office at Victoria Station and was brusquely driven once more to the back of the long queue by impatient and unsympathetic travellers. However, there can be little doubt that he was a clever child. *Of Human Bondage* gives a harsh account of his schooldays and a hardly less dry portrait of himself, under the name of Philip Carey. The boy is credulous and sensitive, but he also has a way with words. When young Maugham could get his tongue round a phrase, it was likely to be a wounding one.

His school career, which might have been expected to culminate with entrance into Cambridge, was interrupted by a lung infection. His guardians must have feared that the disease which had killed both his mother and his aunt was now to destroy the adolescent boy. He was packed off to a tutor in Hyères, one of the first resorts on the Riviera to be patronized by the English. There, at the age of sixteen, he discovered French literature, in particular the stories of Guy de Maupassant.

Above left, long-remembered schooldays in England; Somerset Maugham is fourth from the left among the boys sitting on the ground.

Above, Somerset Maugham in the Fifth Form in 1889, when he was fifteen.

A cubicled dormitory at King's School.

Hyères, the resort in the South of France where Somerset Maugham was sent at the age of sixteen to recover from a lung infection.

Professor Kuno Fischer lecturing at Heidelberg University.

Opposite, Somerset Maugham aged about seventeen.

The Mediterranean air cleared his lungs and he was able to go back to the King's School for his last year. He was still wretched – he never forgot a particularly brutal master – but he was armed with a new, secret weapon: a growing familiarity and ease with words. Whether or not he could get them out, they swarmed easily and eloquently into his mind. If he could but express them, it would be a rare man who would get the better of him.

It was time to consider his profession. The Reverend Henry considered very few vocations suitable for a gentleman. The young Maugham's stammer further limited the choice. Secretly, he had already chosen: he would be a writer. His uncle thought the Church more suitable. Willie neither agreed nor disagreed, for the time being. Decision was postponed by a long stay in Heidelberg, which began in 1891, after he had left the King's School. Maugham was later to regret, or to affect to regret, that he had not been 'properly educated'. But during his nine months in Heidelberg, though he was not a formal member of the University, he attended the lectures of, among others, the brilliant Kuno Fischer, whose speciality was Schopenhauer, that philosopher of misogynistic pessimism and stoic, often witty, pithiness. He also met a young man, Ellingham Brooks, who 'burned with a hard gem-like flame' and whose ardent passion for literature (and doubtless for the young Maugham, who was too innocent to be aware of such an ulterior motive) alerted the public-schoolboy to the power of great writers. Brooks later went to Capri where, a true lotus-eater, he lived for the whole of his long life without ever doing a hand's turn.

Maugham returned to England a young man. He spoke fluent German and he had no mind to enclose himself in the narrow scholastic horizons of an English university. He had already seen too much of the outside world. He had a small income of £150 a year from the father he had supposed so rich, a pittance to be sure, but an independent pittance, and he now felt strong enough openly to resist his

uncle's proposal that he go into the Church. He tried chartered accountancy for a couple of months, hated it and returned to Whitstable. The Vicar was less than delighted to have him on his hands. The local doctor suggested he try medicine. In 1892, he enrolled as a medical student at St Thomas's Hospital, London. He felt no vocation for medicine, but he possessed a strong desire to lead a London life.

While in Heidelberg he had written a biography of Meyerbeer, although he had scant knowledge of his work. This, after its rejection by a publisher, he was wise enough to destroy, but the habit of writing remained. He began secretly to keep a notebook; secretly, because to be a writer was among the many things the Victorian upper-middle-class considered *infra dig*.

He lodged at 11 Vincent Square, Westminster, across the river from the hospital. He was not a dedicated medical student. All the time he could spare was devoted to reading. He passed his exams regularly, however, and in 1893 he became a clerk in the Outpatients Department. Here he began to encounter life at first hand. As for literature, during one particular two-month period of which he happened to keep a record, he read 'Three Shakespeare plays, two volumes of Mommsen's History of Rome, a large part of Lanson's Littérature Française, two or three novels, some of the French classics, a couple of scientific works and an Ibsen play.'

He also frequented the West End theatre. By chance he was given tickets for a couple of good seats for a first night, at the St James's Theatre, in early 1895. It was of *Guy Domville*, Henry James's disastrous and solemn drama. He saw the unfortunate James booed from the stage. On the same night, Oscar Wilde's comedy, *An Ideal Husband*, opened triumphantly round the corner at the Haymarket. A young man of Maugham's acuity can hardly have failed to note on which side a playwright's bread was buttered.

The medical student saw a side of London life which the privileged could contrive to ignore. When Maugham crossed the Thames, he crossed a Lethe the farther bank

A scene from Oscar Wilde's *An Ideal Husband*, which opened in London on 3 January 1895.

A ward in St Thomas's Hospital in the 1890s.

Opposite, Regent Street at night; detail of a painting by Francis Foster, 1897-98.

of which both his Christian uncle and his lawyer brother were happy to forget. In 1895, he spent three weeks as an obstetric clerk in the slums of Lambeth. He was on call night and day, and attended sixty-three confinements, many of them in those dark alleys and courts where, he was able to boast, no policeman would ever dare to venture alone, and where literary gentlemen were not likely to venture in any numbers. He had already begun to sketch out a novel based on his hospital experiences but Liza, the heroine of his first novel, was born of his harsh initiation into the lower depths of Victorian Bermondsey. He would have preferred to write for the theatre. He had been deeply impressed by Ibsen and was already writing plays which 'delved ruthlessly into the secrets of the human soul; few of my characters but suffered from a fatal or venereal disease, and since I was studying medicine I was able to go into some very elegant detail.'

But who would produce the plays of an unknown Ibsenite? In those days the novel was a safer bet. The manuscript of *Liza of Lambeth* was sent to Fisher Unwin, who had previously expressed interest in a novella Maugham had sent him but which was disqualified from publication by being of so uncommercial a length. The publisher's readers were not unstinting in their praise. The low-life of the urban proletariat was not a subject into which the average reader of a novel wished to be thrust too brutally, and there was in the language and action of *Liza of Lambeth* a good measure of life's brutality. Vaughan Nash, the first reader, wrote his report on 4 January 1897:

The writer shows considerable acquaintance with the speech and customs of a certain class of the London poor and if he knew how to use his materials his work might possess a certain value. But this study shows no trace of any such power. Its details, some of which are revolting and, I should suppose, unsuitable for publication, are strung together loosely and there is no touch of romance, no sense of character, and no atmosphere from first to last.... Altogether I feel that as an experiment in realistic writing the story will not do.... But in the event of publication I would suggest that it should be carefully read in view of certain passages which strike me as particularly offensive. The author's capacity for vulgarity on his own account is considerable.

Fisher Unwin was not put off. He may have been skilful in duping writers into signing disadvantageous contracts, but he also had a nose for talent; nor is a capacity for vulgarity always an uncommercial quality in an author. He sent the manuscript to Edward Garnett, whose response was far more positive. Garnett was aware of the growing popularity of the realistic style of fiction originated by Emile Zola and now exemplified in England by Arthur Morrison (*A Child of the Jago*) and Edward Gissing (*Joseph Vance*). He advocated publication; if Unwin did not publish, someone else would. He added a significant P.S.: 'The conversation is remarkably well done.'

Fisher Unwin sought a third opinion. Mr W.H. Chess was no less favourable than Garnett. He also took Vaughan Nash to task:

... a story to 'take or leave'. A process of pruning down would be absurd. If people don't like to read of a love that takes the form of a 'swinging blow to the belly' they won't; if they do, they will. Yet one feels that Mr Maugham knows his people and between those and these there is not a great gulf fixed after all.

Liza of Lambeth was published by Fisher Unwin in the autumn of 1897. Its author was twenty-three and his advance was £20. The notices were not uniformly good. Vaughan Nash had his counterparts in the critical world. *The Athenaeum* found the book 'emphatically unpleasing' and the *Academy* reviewer felt that he had 'taken a mud bath in all the filth of a London street'. *Vanity Fair* said plainly that it was 'dirty'. There were compensations. Basil Wilberforce, who was later to be Archdeacon of Westminster, made Liza the subject of a sermon in the Abbey one Sunday night. Among the congregation was Maugham's kindly Cockney landlady from 11 Vincent Square, just round the corner. And if the critics were not all amiable, Maugham had a taste of the revenge which was to be his consolation throughout his career. The book sold like hot cakes. The first edition was soon exhausted; a second was ordered. William Somerset Maugham was an author. A few weeks later he was also a doctor, a qualified M.R.C.S., L.R.C.P. But there was no medicine like writing.

A modern reader is unlikely to be shocked by *Liza of Lambeth*. The story is simple. Liza works in a factory and lives alone with her widowed, drunken mother in Vere Street, Lambeth. She has a young man, Tom, for whom she does not greatly care. They go on a Bank Holiday outing arranged by the people of Vere Street and there she meets Jim Blakiston, who has recently moved into the street with his wife. She falls in love with Jim, has what she hopes is a secret affair with him and becomes pregnant. But there are no secrets in Vere Street; a fierce fight takes place between Liza and Jim's wife. Liza is badly beaten, has a miscarriage and dies.

The simplicity of the story and the detachment with which it is put down do not conceal a measure of indignation and pity. Liza's vitality is like that of a spring daisy which pushes between the hard slabs of a city pavement and then is crushed by unheeding boots. (Did Bernard Shaw, when he came to create a Cockney flower-girl, subconsciously remember Maugham's heroine and name Eliza Doolittle after her?)

There is a pastoral charm in Maugham's first novel, a charm shot with violence and a relish for cruel realities but instinct also with a tenderness which perhaps came more easily when he considered a society quite alien from his own and the doomed gaiety of those isolated within the harsh picturesqueness of the slum. Had it not been for his field-work as a medical student, he could never have known of such people. But his dry style ('I put down what I had seen and heard as plainly as possible') does not wholly preclude a personal sense of the fragility of beauty and happiness.

Edmund Gosse thought extremely well of *Liza*. In later years he would greet its author with the words, 'Ah my dear Maugham, I so enjoyed your *Liza of Lambeth*. How wise you were never to publish anything else!' The book was talked about and one of the consultants at St Thomas's offered the young author an assistantship, which he refused. Henceforth he would devote himself to literature. It was a decision he was later to say that he regretted. It seems absurd to suppose that he would have preferred a medical career, yet perhaps at the very moment when he might have stepped into the real world, armed with his degree, he retreated, and knew that he had retreated, into the bloodless haven of literature. To be sure, he did not shut out the smells and sounds of the street, but nor did he show any zest for bathing in the mud he had stirred up.

Edmund Gosse, the literary critic who praised Somerset Maugham's first novel, *Liza of Lambeth*.

Liza of Lambeth and the London Maugham described in the novel. *Above,* a drawing by William Nicholson, 1898, of the 'Liza' type. *Right and opposite,* street scenes from Lambeth, Bermondsey and Westminster.

His uncle, the Vicar of Whitstable, died in the year *Liza of Lambeth* was published. His aunt, the patient Sophia, had died five years earlier. The Reverend Henry MacDonald erected a pulpit in her memory, which still stands in the parish church, and then he remarried. The whole of his modest estate (it was valued at £1,677) went to his widow. In *Of Human Bondage*, Philip's uncle leaves everything to him. In fact, all that Maugham derived from his uncle was a letter he himself discovered and which had been written to the Vicar by Edith Maugham on the occasion of William's birth. It ended with the hope that the child would 'become a soldier in Christ's Faith and be all the days of his life God-fearing, humble and pious'.

The Vicar's funeral was well attended. There were Freemasons with sprigs of acacia, for Henry MacDonald was a Past Provincial Grand Chaplain, and there was William Somerset Maugham, who a fortnight before had sent the Reverend gentleman a copy of his first novel. Had it perhaps been the last straw? He can hardly have failed to hope so. Yet he was later to suspect that there were virtues of humour and even of a desiccated affection in his uncle's attitude to him. 'A parson is paid to preach – not to practise,' he had noted among the sayings of the Vicar, a remark redolent of a cynicism which may have shocked, but perhaps also instructed, the young man.

The second novel was, traditionally, difficult to write, especially if you had had a success with the first. Maugham was seduced by some advice offered by Andrew Lang, then at the peak of his influence as a man of letters: young men should not attempt to deal with the complexities of life around them but should write historical novels. Their lack of worldly knowledge would not then blight their freshness. Would Lang have included among the innocent a young writer with Maugham's knowledge of Bermondsey and of the wards in which he had seen men and women die and children suffer the agonies of diphtheria? How docile in the face of confident advice the young can be! Already, one cannot but suspect, Maugham had had more

The romantic Spain, which had such a deep and liberating effect on the young Maugham; a painting by John Singer Sargent called *El Jaleo*.

Seville about the time when Maugham first went there.

experience of reality than Andrew Lang, but he addressed himself to an historical novel with industrious earnestness.

He chose to go to Spain. He had already been twice to Capri, during his vacations from medical school; he liked the South, he had no difficulty with languages and he found there a *douceur de vivre* missing under grim English skies. He established himself in Seville, grew a moustache, smoked cigars and took lessons in the guitar. He also fell in love with a girl whose identity remains shadowy but whose dark hair and flashing eyes make her sound like uncommonly good casting for Carmen. At all events, he was happy.

So to myself Seville means ten times more than it can mean to others. I came to it after weary years in London, heartsick with much hoping, my mind dull with drudgery; and it seemed a land of freedom. There I became at last conscious of my youth, and it seemed a *belvedere* on a new life. How can I forget the delight of my wandering in the Sierpes, released at length from all imprisoning ties, watching the various movements as though it were a stage-play, yet half afraid that the falling curtain would bring back reality?

He travelled widely, on horseback, riding the roads of Andalucia, gazing at new sights with old eyes; his vision was deeply influenced by George Borrow and Prosper Merimée. He did not find it easy to be free of literary influences. He went to Granada and took a room near the Alhambra. Later he was to write, in *Don Fernando*, of a certain young man who went to that city for the first time.

On the night of his arrival, after dinner, too excited to stay in, he went down to the town. Here, because he was twenty-four and also perhaps a little because he thought the gesture suited to the occasion, he had himself directed to a brothel. He picked out a girl of whom he could remember nothing afterwards but that she had large green eyes in a pallid face. He was struck by their colour, for it was that which old Spanish poets and story-tellers were always giving to their heroines, and since it is a colour very seldom seen in Spain the commentators have opined that when the writers talked of green they meant something else. But here it was. When the girl stripped the young man was taken aback to see that she was still a child.

'You look very young to be in a place like this,' he said. 'How old are you?'
'Thirteen.'
'What made you come here?'
'Hambre,' she answered. 'Hunger.'

The young man suffered from a sensibility that was doubtless excessive. The tragic word stabbed him. Giving her money (he was poor and could not afford much) he told the girl to dress up again, and, all passion spent, slowly climbed the hill and went to bed.

Most of his nine months in Andalucia was spent in Seville, that enchanting city of white houses, orange trees, flowering patios and black wrought-iron. He wrote a travel book about Spain which he later cannibalized for *The Land of the Blessed Virgin* (not published until 1905) and a manuscript provisionally entitled 'The Artistic Temperament of Stephen Carey' which he elected not to submit for publication and which was, of course, also cannibalized when he came to write *Of Human Bondage*. The next published work was earnest of his respect for Andrew Lang; it was entitled 'The Making of a Saint' and it was the fruit of his vacations spent in Capri and spare time spent in the British Museum. If the story was set in Italy, it was conceived in London and composed with more application than verve. Maugham himself said that Fisher Unwin must have been dismayed when he received it.

The story is set in Forlì and the *donnée* comes from the eighth book of Machiavelli's *History of Florence*; the heroine is Caterina Sforza and the plot a melodramatic confection of blood, passion and perfunctory piety. The epigraph was of four lines of Italian verse, with a translation; it was one thing to listen to one's betters, like Mr Lang, but one's readers were not to be left without a crib. A certain considerate condescension, like his dissident deference to those well established in the world, was to stay with him all his life. John Halliwell, the *raisonneur* in his play, *A Man of Honour*, written in 1898, put it this way,

You know, men and women without end have snapped their fingers at society and laughed at it, and for a while they thought they had the better of it. But all the time society was quietly smiling up its sleeve, and suddenly it put out an iron hand – and scrunched them up.

Opposite, nineteenth-century view of the Alhambra, Granada.

Oscar Wilde in 1894, at the height of his career, with Lord Alfred Douglas.

The Wilde scandal evoked strong public feeling; this picture of a prehistoric monster was sent to Wilde anonymously.

In that same year Oscar Wilde published *The Ballad of Reading Gaol*. Maugham had first gone to the theatre when Wilde's scintillating and scandalous fame was at its height. He too had tried to toss off brilliant epigrams (or, more often, settled for writing down later what he wished he had said at the time) and he had seen Wilde's star falter at the zenith and plunge into the gutter. A lifelong caution with regard to homosexuality seemed to sort ill with a Gallic frankness in matters of more normal sexuality. Can one believe that his desire to make a success in England did not go hand in hand with a fear of English hypocrisy and vindictiveness?

Maugham continued to write plays, but it was to be ten more years before one of them was produced. In the meanwhile he published a number of novels and stories, with no large success. After a volume of stories, *Orientations*, he parted company with Fisher Unwin and went to Hutchinson, who brought out *The Hero* in 1901. It was the first of his books to carry his father's Moorish device, which was to become his trademark. On this occasion it was printed upside down; certainly it brought him no luck. *The Hero* took a cynical, or humane, look at the Boer War and the jingoism of those who never left England and had no idea of the realities of warfare. James Parsons, the hero, wins the V.C. as a result of a hot-headed act that results in the death of a man who might otherwise have survived. On his return to England he is unable to subscribe to the cosy sexual and religious morality of a country still convinced that God is an English gentleman. James falls in love with a Eurasian widow of a major in his regiment, who rejects him for a richer man. Unable to face a lifetime with the nice, dull girl whom he knew before he went to South Africa, he ends by committing suicide. The story is both glum and unsatisfactory; it pleased neither the public nor the critics. It emphasized once again, however, Maugham's unhappy apprehension that it was not easy to fight society and there was a measure of courage in his disdain for a jingoism whose force he never underestimated. He once defined tolerance as another name for indifference. Perhaps he was indifferent to the fortunes of the British; they did not, after all, come first with him as they did with themselves. If his tolerance lacked passion, it was not without a sort of rueful indignation.

Mrs Craddock, the first of his novels to be published by William Heinemann, appeared in 1902. (He was to publish his last volume with the same house exactly sixty years later.) Once again the theme is the crass conformity of English provincial life. Bertha Ley, who married Edward Craddock, one of her tenants, is the cousin of Miss Ley, the detached *raisonneuse* whose persona is the first to have the Maughamian quality of detached worldliness that he was to wish on Willie Ashenden and finally on the character whom he called Mr Maugham. Edward Craddock appears to have those vigorous qualities which have come to be associated with Lawrentian gamekeepers, but if he is sexually attractive he is also coarse and stupid. The child Bertha bears him is stillborn (so much for the regeneration of the middle class through an infusion of peasant blood) and the marriage ends in Bertha's disillusionment and Craddock's death while riding a dangerous horse he is too vain to fear. Miss Ley, who has kept her detachment and her money, also maintains a sanity which Bertha, victim of her own passionate folly, has all but lost. The book was not a success; the first edition was remaindered. Yet Maugham, who was now sharing a flat near Victoria Station in London, did not remain without some social recognition. Thanks to Mrs Wilberforce, the wife of the Archdeacon, he met people in smart society. He was invited to country-houses for the week-end; Miss Ley herself is said to have been modelled on Mrs G. W. Steevens, the widow of the *Daily Mail* correspondent who died at the Siege of Ladysmith. She was a considerable figure in Edwardian London and her house, Merton Abbey, where Nelson had lived with Emma Hamilton, was a summer rendezvous for writers and artists. The poverty of which Maugham later claimed he was once a victim probably affected him more at this time than at any other. He was not poor as the people of Vere Street were poor, but he experienced the charmless anxieties of those who move among the well-off without being well-off themselves. He was embarrassed about tips and he was unable to return hospitality. He was shy, but he had no small idea of himself. His lack of affluence did not leave him hungry; it left him ashamed. He shared the Pimlico flat with a friend whom he had met in Germany, Walter Payne. Payne, on Maugham's account, was a successful womanizer. When he had finished with a woman he passed her on to his shy flatmate. Maugham's sexual encounters were frequent, apparently, but they were with Payne's pickups and were quite without love on either side. If they were not commercial transactions, they were very close to being so. This period of his life was more wretched than romantic and it lasted until he was almost thirty.

In 1903 came a happy omen. His first play was performed by the Stage Society. It was called *A Man of Honour*. The Stage Society mounted plays of an uncommercial nature and it was a great feather in a young man's cap to have his play put on at one of their Sunday-night performances. There was no run, in the usual sense, but it was the best shop-window in London for new talent. The play had been written in Rome, in 1898, and Maugham rehashed part of it in his next novel, *The Merry-Go-Round*. *A Man of Honour* is, so far as plot goes, *Mrs Craddock* in reverse: a young solicitor makes a barmaid pregnant, marries her out of a sense of honour and finds himself in a prison of vulgarity and mediocrity from which the wretched girl's suicide alone delivers him. A *succès d'estime* was followed by a production at the Avenue Theatre, where a revised ending brought no larger success.

Maugham was during this period, perhaps for the only time in his life, associated with the more advanced and even daring authors of the day. He became co-editor

The Café Royal, London, in its Edwardian heyday; a painting by William Orpen.

with Laurence Housman of a short-lived literary magazine, *The Venture, An Annual of Art and Literature*. Among the contributors were John Masefield, G. K. Chesterton, Thomas Hardy, Richard Garnett, Havelock Ellis, Edmund Gosse, Alfred Noyes, Arthur Symons and James Joyce. Among his other literary friends were George Bernard Shaw, Max Beerbohm and Frank Harris of whom he later said that he wrote several short stories which were so good that people said he could not possibly have written them himself. Maugham found Harris good company until the day came when Maugham was rich and Harris was poor. Even then he was good company but expensive. That Maugham had elected to become an editor is a measure alike of his modest fame and, perhaps, of his sense of frustration as an author. Writers rarely edit except in moments of disillusion with their own literary fortunes. *The Venture* failed and Maugham quit London, for Paris. He had always loved the city and he found congenial company among the writers and artists who frequented Le Chat Blanc, a café-restaurant in the rue d'Odessa. He lived near the Lion de Belfort and dined often with the rowdy expatriates who argued and postured around the sinister, magnetic figure of Aleister Crowley. He there met his lifelong friend Gerald

A view of the rue d'Odessa, Paris, in the early twentieth century.

Gerald Kelly, the artist, who was among the lasting friends Maugham made during his 1903 visit to Paris.

Kelly, the engaging, talkative Irish Old Etonian who was later to be President of the Royal Academy. There was also Arnold Bennett (doubtless gathering material for *The Old Wives' Tale* which Maugham was to hail promptly, if with surprise, as a masterpiece), George Moore, Clive Bell, James Wilson Morrice, a whole gallery of Bohemians free of the need to tip supercilious servants or to do the right thing.

Not the least interesting was Roderic O'Conor, an Irish painter of a surly disposition who disliked Maugham but told him much of Paul Gauguin; the character of Charles Strickland in *The Moon and Sixpence* was perhaps an amalgam of the two men. Crowley, the Great Beast at the overblown height of his gargantuan insolence and self-confidence, fascinated and perhaps intimidated the always fastidious Maugham. A portrait of him, and of the habitués of Le Chat Blanc, was to appear in *The Magician*, a 'very dull and stupid book' (in the author's accurate words), full of cooked-up horrors, which was published in 1908. During this time, more than any other, Maugham found himself in the company of painters. It is sometimes suggested (and Maugham himself may have been responsible for the suggestion) that his own famous collection of Impressionists was shrewdly begun then, when a Sisley or a Van Gogh might have been picked up for the price of the meal which, in his short story, 'The Luncheon', an impecunious young author buys for a greedy visiting lady in a Paris restaurant, but the truth is more prosaic: Maugham seems to have bought very few of his Impressionists until the Second World War, though his love of painting was deep and constant.

In 1904, he returned to London, possibly for the publication of *The Merry-Go-Round*, an experimental novel which again figured Miss Ley as the *raisonneuse* of three distinct stories. It cannot be said that the experimentation was of a high order. It was evidence perhaps more of his uncertainty as an artist (nothing had gone right since *Liza of Lambeth*) than of any confident assault on conventional literary forms. He was so dismayed by Heinemann's failure to sell the book that he was on the point of leaving them. He left his literary agent, William Maurice Colles, instead: it was he who had persuaded a reluctant Heinemann to publish the novel and, in Maugham's view, expressed in a letter from Capri later, he might 'just as well have thrown it into the Thames'. Arnold Bennett recommended J. B. Pinker, who agreed to handle *The Bishop's Apron*, which was sent to Chapman and Hall and published in 1906. It was a rehash of a play, *Loaves and Fishes*, which was eventually produced in 1912, and satirized the political and sexual machinations of a worldly and ambitious cleric. Maugham said later that he wrote it in order to get enough money to entertain a lady with a taste for luxury (had she visited him in Paris, one wonders?) and that by the time it was finished, 'the passion that I had thought would last forever was extinct'. He no longer wished to spend it on a woman, so, in the steps of Flaubert, he 'went to Egypt instead'.

In July 1904, during Maugham's stay in London, his brother Henry killed himself. Like his brother Charles, who followed his father by practising in Paris, Harry was a solicitor, but he wished also to be a writer. He published a verse drama, *The Husband of Poverty*, on the life of St Francis of Assisi and was on the fringes of the *Yellow Book* world which had already lost its spring and its summer with the passing of Beardsley and the humiliation of Wilde. He had come to the first night of *A Man of Honour*, in a shabby blue suit, when the rest of the company was in full evening dress, and saluted the author with the brave words, 'I'm glad to hear that my little brother has had some success at last.' He himself was never to have any. On reading the manuscript of *Liza of Lambeth*, he had advised Willie against a literary career, but it may have been less out of sibling malice than through his usual misreading of the public taste. He was a lovable as well as a sad man, and it was only after his ghastly suicide that his young brother realized how much he had loved him. He had swallowed nitric acid and was discovered in agony by Willie, at his lodgings in Cadogan Street. He was rushed in a cab to St Thomas's, but there was nothing to be done. He had swallowed the acid three days previously and had been alone, in agony, ever since. 'I'm sure', Maugham told his nephew Robin many years later, 'it wasn't only failure that made him kill himself. It was the life he led.' Perhaps Maugham's lifelong terror of being branded as a homosexual was reinforced by the pathetic end of his aesthete brother.

The failure of *Loaves and Fishes* found Maugham's fortunes at their lowest ebb. He thought he would have to go back to medicine and considered becoming a ship's doctor. His income was not much over £250 a year. It is not surprising that *The*

Magician (written at this nadir in his fortunes) strove for sensation. It caused none and limped gauchely in pursuit of the kind of *frisson* so effortlessly achieved by J. K. Huysmans in *Là Bas*, on which it is clearly, if inadequately, modelled. Aleister Crowley's reaction was splendid and typical:

Late in 1908 I picked up a book. The title attracted me strongly, *The Magician*. The author, bless my soul! No other than my old and valued friend, William Somerset Maugham, my nice young doctor whom I remembered so well from the dear old days of the *Chat Blanc*. So he had really written a book – who would have believed it! I carried it off to Scott's. In my excitement, I actually paid for it. I think I ate two dozen oysters and a pheasant, and drank a bottle of No. 111, one of the happiest champagnes in the famous – can you say 'caterer's'? Yes: – I mean caterer's cellar. Yes, I did myself proud, for the Magician, Oliver Haddo, was Aleister Crowley; his house 'Skene' was Boleskine. The hero's witty remarks were, many of them, my own. He had, like Arnold Bennett, not spared his shirt cuff.... I like Maugham well enough personally, though many people resent a curious trick which he has of saying spiteful things about everybody. I always feel that he, like myself, makes such remarks without malice, for the sake of their cleverness.... Well, Maugham had had his fun with me; I would have mine with him. I wrote an article for Vanity Fair (December 30th, 1908) in which I disclosed the method by which the book had been manufactured and gave parallel passages. Frank Harris [the editor] would not believe that I was serious. He swore I must be making it up. He could not believe that any man would have the impudence to publish such strings of plagiarism.... Maugham took my riposte in good part. We met by chance a few weeks later and he merely remarked that there were many thefts besides those which I had pointed out.

Luckily, by 1908, when it was actually published, the success or failure of *The Magician* was of small importance. For, one morning in October 1907, at the age of thirty-three, Maugham woke up and found himself famous.

It was the morning after the première of *Lady Frederick*. Of the six full-length plays he had written, only *A Man of Honour* had been performed, and that briefly. But in the autumn season of 1907, a play failed at the Royal Court; the manager, Otho Stuart, was desperate for a replacement. He accepted *Lady Frederick*, which was offered to him by Golding Bright, Maugham's enthusiastic dramatic agent, as a stopgap for six weeks. Its success was such that within a year Maugham had four plays running in the West End (*Lady Frederick*, *Jack Straw*, *Mrs Dot* and, less successfully, *The Explorer*). Bernard Partridge, in a famous cartoon in *Punch*, depicted an apprehensive William Shakespeare gazing at the playbills of the young prodigy. It was the fruit of long years of frustration that made him so suddenly prodigious.

Most women, Max Beerbohm once said, are not as young as they are painted. Maugham's overnight success came of making the same point, in three acts. The fame of *Lady Frederick* was due above all to one outrageous scene. The young Marquess of Mareston, having proposed insistently to Lady Frederick, a much older woman, is saved from a disastrous engagement by her own stratagem. She invites him into her presence early enough in the day to witness the application of her false hair and make-up. She then tells him that he should learn his lesson and never marry an older woman. He bows out gracefully and Lady Frederick makes an alliance with a man as mature and as worldly as herself. The mixture of realism (it was not at first easy to persuade Ethel Irving to enact Lady Frederick's disillusioning toilette on stage) and

A *Punch* cartoon, June 1908, at the time when Maugham had four plays running simultaneously in London.

MAYFAIR.

WITH POSSESSION.

THE PARTICULARS AND CONDITIONS OF SALE

OF THE VERY

Long Leasehold Residence

No. 6, CHESTERFIELD STREET,

·MAYFAIR.

Held for over

800 YEARS UNEXPIRED,

At a merely nominal Ground Rent, and is thus almost equivalent to

FREEHOLD.

WHICH WILL BE OFFERED FOR SALE BY AUCTION BY MESSRS.

Arber, Rutter, Waghorn & Brown

At the Mart, Tokenhouse Yard, Bank, E.C.,

On THURSDAY, the 20th day of MAY, 1909,

At ONE o'Clock precisely (unless previously sold by private treaty).

Printed Particulars and Conditions of Sale may be had of Messrs. SIMPSON, CULLINGFORD, PARTINGTON and HOLLAND, Solicitors, 85, Gracechurch Street, E.C.; at the Mart; and, with Orders to View, at the Auctioneers' Offices,

1, Mount Street, Berkeley Square, London, W.

Telephone—GERRARD 1020.

For-sale notice of the house Maugham bought in 1909.

Overleaf, left above, a scene from *Mrs Dot* (Marie Tempest in the centre), when it was running at the Comedy Theatre in 1908.

Left below, A Man of Honour; photographs of Maugham's play in *The Tatler,* 23 March 1904.

Right, the Gerald Kelly portrait of Somerset Maugham at the height of his success as a playwright.

hard-boiled sentiment was to serve Maugham well during the twenty-six years of his theatrical career. If the comparison with Shakespeare was premature (on being informed of it, his brother Frederick, already a successful lawyer, replied that he had only one piece of advice, 'On no account attempt the sonnets'), William Somerset Maugham was now abruptly and forever a man of substantial income; a single week's royalties were as much as he had earned in a whole year before *Lady Frederick.* He was not surprised by success; he rejoiced in it. He looked for a house in Mayfair; he went to a good tailor; he was elected to the Garrick Club (in 1909) and he had his portrait painted by Gerald Kelly. The days of taking a back seat in Le Chat Blanc were gone, forever. So too were the days when he was rated highly by intellectuals; if money adorned him in the eyes of the world, it damned him in the sight of the intelligentsia.

Maugham's Mayfair house at
6 Chesterfield Street.

His pleasure in popularity did not lead him to remove a certain astringency from the plays which were now given such prompt productions, but having discovered the trick of pleasing the public, he was not about to endanger the favour it had taken him so long to acquire. He still said some hard things, but he said them charmingly. The epigram is a useful weapon; it enables one to be both sardonic and entertaining and it is most appreciated by the very people at whom its barbs are aimed. Maugham might fairly have been accused of trying to have things both ways. Max Beerbohm, whose experience of the theatre had been that of a reluctant, if often perspicuous critic, once remonstrated with him, saying that Maugham had a mind too delicate, a sensitiveness too refined, ever to succeed in 'the vulgar scramble of the stage'. Maugham remarked dryly: 'He little knew.' But Max did, in a way, know. After four hectic years of success, Maugham tired, though only temporarily, of the theatre. In 1911, when he was comfortably established in a town house at 6 Chesterfield Street, Mayfair, and had become a host to all the smartest people who passed through or lived in London, he quit the theatre for more than two years and wrote another novel. Its title was taken from one of the sections which compose Spinoza's *Ethics*: *Of Human Bondage*.

I was but just firmly established as a popular playwright when I began to be obsessed by the teeming memories of my past life. The loss of my mother and then the break-up of my home, the wretchedness of my first years at school for which my French childhood had so ill-prepared me and which my stammering made so difficult, the delight of those easy, monotonous and exciting days in Heidelberg, when I first entered upon the intellectual life, the irksomeness of my few years at the hospital and the thrill of London; it all came back to me so pressingly, in my sleep, on my walks, when I was rehearsing plays, when I was at a party, it became such a burden to me that I made up my mind that I could only regain my peace by writing it all down in the form of a novel.

Of Human Bondage is a *Bildungsroman* written in a harshly realistic style, with little formal structure or plot development, though with a wealth of incident. The autobiographical element is paramount. We meet Philip Carey as a small boy of six years whose mother has just died, leaving him alone in the world. He is sent to live with his aunt and uncle, the Vicar of Blackstable. Philip does not have the stammer which so tortured Willie; he has a club-foot, an even more inexorable brand. He is tormented at school (these scenes have a cruel immediacy) and repressed at home. He is sexually uncertain and personally timid. Having a credulous nature, forever being ensnared by stronger characters, however bogus they turn out to be, and no clear idea of what he wants to be, only of what he wants to escape, he endures many disillusionments. He goes to Paris and studies painting. Deterred by the grim price of failure, however, he eventually returns to London to become a doctor. There ensues the most memorable portion of the novel. Philip, living in miserable circumstances, is drawn into a degrading passion for a waitress, Mildred, whose mean and unprepossessing personality utterly enslaves and nearly ruins him; he is forced by her exigence to renounce medical school and become a shop assistant. It is only when Philip's uncle dies that he is left enough money to resume his medical studies, qualify, fall in love with the pretty daughter of a kindly couple who have befriended him, and foresee a happy, liberated future as a country doctor.

One of Maugham's masters at King's
School, Canterbury, the cruelties of
which appear in the early chapters of
Of Human Bondage.

Bette Davis as Mildred in the 1934 film version of *Of Human Bondage*. 'She was very anaemic. Her thin lips were pale, of a faint green colour, without a touch of red even in the cheeks.'

The conclusion is an acknowledged piece of wish-fulfilment, a happy ending tacked on to a work of such obstinate gloom that the public might have been forgiven for liking it no better than it did the books which preceded the success of *Lady Frederick*. Yet there is an astonishing drive and vitality to the course of the whole long novel. This is due partly to the panoramic canvas, with episodes in Paris and Capri and Heidelberg, partly to the variety of vivid characters, not least the enigmatic Cronshaw who alerts Philip to the nihilistic message concealed in a Persian carpet, that 'life has no meaning', and above all to the hideous fascination of Mildred, with her blanched complexion, her flat chest and her greedy cunning.

It has been suggested that this androgynous character was perhaps, in Maugham's own life, not a girl at all, but a Cockney homosexual prostitute of the kind that ruined Wilde. Blackmail was a constant danger with such men. No one has given any convincing account of Mildred's specific origin, but it is interesting to note that in 'The Artistic Temperament of Stephen Carey', the draft which Maugham wrote during his time in Seville, the girl who occupied Mildred's place in the plot was of a far less odious disposition. He called her Rose; the same name, transmuted to Rosie, was to be given, much later, to the heroine whom Willie Ashenden loves. Mildred may, of course, have been based on one of Walter Payne's less charming semi-prostitute cast-offs. If so, her place in Willie's plot had already been, so to speak, booked.

The world of *Lady Frederick* and *Mrs Dot*, where forms were all and where bad behaviour was tolerated only so long as it did not upset the social order, the world in which the play of Maugham's well-spoken wit chimed with the complacency of an upper class that had plenty to smile about, came to an end in August 1914. By the time the proofs of *Of Human Bondage* were in his hand, Maugham was in Flanders. He was forty; it was a long time since he had had any practical medical experience, but he was able to volunteer as an ambulance driver and dresser. By chance Desmond

MacCarthy was in the same unit. MacCarthy's later account of their meeting shows with what suspicion Maugham was already regarded by the élite. It also makes handsome amends:

A scene in a little bedroom at Malo near Dunkirk comes back to me: a thick roll of proofs had arrived for him; he had corrected them and the long strips were lying on the bed ... although I was short of something to read, my interest in them was confined to noticing how very few corrections he had made. When I remarked on it, he replied that he always went over his work carefully before he sent it to the printer. 'Ah,' I thought, 'he's as businesslike as a novelist as he is as a playwright. The itch for perfection doesn't trouble him; the adequate will do. I suppose the book will sell.' And these were the proofs of *Of Human Bondage*! A novel which, together with *The Old Wives' Tale, A Farewell to Arms, Kipps, Babbitt* and a few others, will float on the stream of time when the mass of modern realistic fiction is sediment at the bottom.

Maugham had already, before the outbreak of war, met the woman who was to be his wife. Syrie Wellcome was the daughter of Dr Thomas Barnardo, the founder of Barnardo's homes for abandoned children and orphans. They met by chance, in the winter of 1913, when one of a theatre party dropped out and Maugham was invited to replace him. She was a very pretty woman, always beautifully dressed, in her middle thirties, and she lived separately from her allegedly complaisant husband, who belonged to the famous pharmaceutical family. Maugham was proud of her and was gratified to be known as her lover. Syrie moved in the smartest circles; she was used to dining at Ciro's and dancing at the Four Hundred. She was emancipated enough to want to have a child by Maugham and determined enough to prevail upon him to agree. The immediate result was a miscarriage which so depressed her that she suggested they abandon their liaison. Maugham did not wish to do so, and it continued. That Syrie loved him seems beyond doubt and that he, at this time, was willing to challenge the society whose power he fully recognized and have a child by another man's wife argues a certain mild courage and the conclusion that he must, in his way, have been in love.

We shall come later to his relationship with the woman he called Rosie in *Cakes and Ale* and to whom he claimed to have proposed marriage during a trip to America in the summer of 1914, but however much Syrie's dominant personality ensnared him, there was plainly no reluctance and no lack of desire on his part. The memoir *Looking Back* is notoriously as malicious as it is uncorroborated, but not even the bitterness of old age can conceal Syrie's enchanting, if tenacious, character. She was due to join him in Capri (where he was staying with Gerald Kelly) when war broke out and he asked Winston Churchill, with whom he had a golfing and personal friendship dating from Merton Abbey days, to find him a job. Nothing much came of this and so he went with the Ambulance Unit to France.

Whatever the ins and outs of his emotional life, it was certainly something of a relief to be free of entanglements. Maugham was not a callous man; he observed with pity and dismay the sufferings of the wounded and the inanity of the society ladies who did them a favour by looking after them. He saw a man with lung damage given soup by a woman too self-important to heed the words of a doctor who said that she would drown him, which she proceeded to do. Yet there were dividends in the world's calamity. He was dragged from his comfortable rut; he had no

The Cloth Hall, Ypres, in May 1916,
after it had been shelled by the Germans.

An ambulance unit at the Front in 1915.

responsibilities and no decisions to make. He was on the road, notebook in hand, eyes open, with neither dinner engagements to keep nor ladies to entertain. Despite nearly being killed when a shell exploded where he had been standing a moment earlier, against the wall of the Cloth Hall at Ypres, Maugham found the Continent a liberation.

He was given leave in 1915 and went to Rome. Syrie met him there. They took a house. Maugham wrote and played golf. Syrie lived with him. They were largely alone together; there was no society. She told Willie of her life and of the men in it. He was diverted and instructed: the play *Our Betters* was suggested to him by her adventures. He set about writing it. Syrie became pregnant once more.

Maugham did not rejoin the Ambulance Unit. He and Syrie returned to London. There, at a dinner-party, he met the man he called R, whose mistress was a friend of Syrie's. In this way, on his account at least, Maugham was recruited into Military Intelligence. His knowledge of languages and of the European scene made him excellent casting to replace an agent in Geneva who had lost his nerve. Meanwhile there was a period of waiting, and of drama. For Syrie's husband, Henry Wellcome, whose complaisance had been taken for granted by Maugham, now decided to divorce her. He was twenty-six years older than she and it had never been much of a marriage. A marriage, however, it was; and Syrie had maintained, so Maugham had always insisted, that there was no question of Wellcome turning nasty. He did so now. Maugham was cited as co-respondent. The child that Syrie had conceived in Rome was lost, but a man of honour was, in those days, committed to marry a woman in whose divorce he was named. Every day, thousands of men were dying on the Western (and the Eastern) Front, but the code of civilized humbug still obtained in fashionable London. Syrie held Maugham to its provisions by an exigence both distressing and understandable, even on Maugham's scarcely unbiased account. She was frightened; she rehearsed suicide; she made scenes; and she loved him.

It was probably no great hardship that duty sent him to Lucerne, for the ugly machinery of divorce had started; it was no time to be in London. From Lucerne he took up his posting in Geneva. He was supposed to be a literary gentleman and he claimed to be engaged in writing a play. Since the best cover is always the truth, he set about writing *The Unattainable*, a light comedy produced with considerable success in 1916. Syrie joined him for a while, but Geneva had few charms for her. Maugham was working on his play and when he was not, he was away on mysterious missions. Willie Ashenden was born of these experiences.

When he had completed his tour of duty in Geneva, he went first to London and then to New York. The decree absolute had not come through on Syrie's divorce; they could not yet have married. *Our Betters* was to have its first production in the U.S. (most of the female adventurers in the play are American) and it was natural that Maugham should go to supervise it. Lillie Langtry was on the steamer. She was in her sixties, the famous Jersey Lily, but still beautiful. He found her short upper lip very expressive, though he was saddened at the transience of her beauty. She had once had archdukes at her feet and was now proposing to go to New York dance-halls where you paid the men fifty cents to dance with you. The same woman said that a certain Freddie Gebhardt had once been 'the most celebrated man in two hemispheres'. Why? (Maugham had never heard of him.) 'Because I loved him,' she said. After he had been in New York a few weeks, Syrie cabled that she was coming to join him. When she did so, he greeted her with the news that he now intended to set off for Tahiti. She was not pleased. He was firm. He was an author; he needed to collect material for his book on Gauguin and when he came back he would marry her. She 'resigned herself to it'.

That Maugham should have cooled off Syrie is not entirely extraordinary. He had been flattered by her attentions and by the love of an attractive and fashionable woman. But he was morbidly afraid of being trapped. He had written on this theme in *A Man of Honour* nearly twenty years before. He thought Syrie independent and now here she was round his neck. He reacted with cold propriety. He did the right thing; he was damned if he would do more. Syrie's pursuit of him was touching, but it was not wise. Any writer of social comedy could have told her that the importunate woman of the world is not a sympathetic figure. But there was more to it than that. For behind the scenes was another actor. Maugham had met him in France when he too was a member of the Ambulance Unit. His name was Gerald Haxton.

Haxton was a young American, in his early twenties. He was, in the words of Robin Maugham, 'wayward, feckless and brave'. He was also amusing and outrageous. He was a drinker and he was homosexual. Earlier, in 1915, while on leave in London, he had been arrested and charged with gross indecency. The case was tried before Mr Justice Humphreys and Haxton was acquitted. The judge did not conceal his dissent from this verdict. The English Establishment is not entirely governed by the decisions of twelve good men and naïve. A few years later Haxton was declared an undesirable alien and he was never again to be allowed into England.

Such was the companion with whom Maugham set out for the South Seas. It is difficult to say whether Haxton was Maugham's first homosexual passion. He declared, in *Looking Back*, that he had had no such experiences at his public school; he was unable to understand, during his time in Heidelberg, what motive there could be for the interest certain young men showed in him. He had had a number of mistresses, but it is clear that 'sexual congress' had not brought him any great pleasure. Haxton liberated him from a shame which he may well not even have recognized. And at the very time when the war offered him a certain kind of freedom, Syrie's divorce was a catastrophic twist in fate's plot. He took his revenge in a brutal way. He married her in New Jersey on his return from Tahiti and he gave her a child (Liza, whom he surely loved in his fashion), but he wrote about her in such a way that she sounds a scheming, demanding shrew. That reading of her character was partial, to say the least, but how else can she have seemed to a man whose whole sexual nature had been changed (or revealed to him) by a passion which was both fresh and exciting? Decency might have called for an explanation, but honour called for something else: a marriage which was never happy and could end in only one way. Fear must also have played its part in Maugham's concession to Syrie's hopes, for she was a woman with powerful connections in the world of the higher gossip. How could Maugham be frank about Haxton? In his mind it must have seemed certain that Syrie would betray his secret and render him ridiculous, even odious, in the eyes of his fellow countrymen. London was not necessarily his love, but it was his

great market. He split his bets and his personality. He married Syrie and divorced himself. Only his cynicism endured as a reconciling factor.

The South Seas had been a revelation, and not merely because of Haxton's company. It was Maugham's first substantial journey outside the Western Hemisphere. He visited Honolulu (whores cost a dollar, he noted) and Samoa, Fiji, Tonga and Tahiti. The sun did not always shine. At Pago Pago it rained incessantly. It was on that island that he heard of a Miss Thompson (her name actually appeared on a ship's list of the time) and conceived the story he called 'Rain'. A missionary and his wife were of the same company.

She spoke of the depravity of the natives [in the Gilberts] in a voice nothing could hush, but with a vehement, unctuous horror; she described their marriage customs as obscene beyond description. She said that when they first went to the Gilberts it was impossible to find a single 'good girl' in any of the villages.

The tone of vintage Maugham is unmistakable. He had stumbled into a territory that he was to make his own. It turned out, coincidentally, to be a gold-mine. What he enjoyed was not only the Pacific, sometimes calm and brilliantly blue, sometimes as grey as the Atlantic but always wonderfully solitary, but also the anonymity. He had once cursed his bad luck, but success also created its burdens. The life of a

Jeanne Eagels in the original New York production of *Rain*, 1922.

Gloria Swanson and Lionel Barrymore in the first film version, called *Sadie Thompson*, 1928.

celebrity was agreeable, but it was not the real thing. In the South Pacific, among whores and derelicts, among colonists and Chinese, he found a world as naked to his clinical eye as specimens in the dissecting-room. And which of them knew who W. Somerset Maugham was? In Tahiti, he made notes *sur place* for a book about Gauguin, whom Roderic O'Conor had once boasted of *almost* accompanying to this very spot. By chance he discovered that somewhere in the bush was a hut where Gauguin, being ill, had spent some time and, during his convalescence, had painted.

I hired a car, and with a companion drove about till my driver sighted the hut. I got out and walked along a narrow path till I came to it. Half a dozen children were playing on the stoop. A man, presumably their father, strolled out and when I told him what I wanted to see asked me to come in. There were three doors; the lower part of each was of wooden panels and the upper of panes of glass held together by strips of wood. The man told me that Gauguin had painted three pictures on the glass panes. The children had scratched away the painting on two of the doors and were just starting on the third. It represented Eve, nude, with the apple in her hand. I asked the man if he would sell it. 'I should have to buy a new door,' he said. 'How much would that cost?' I asked him. 'Two hundred francs,' he answered. I said I would give him that and he took it with pleasure. We unscrewed the door and with my companion carried it to the car and drove back to Papeete. In the evening another man came to see me and said the door was half his. He asked me for two hundred francs more which I gladly gave him. I had the wooden panel sawn off the frame and, taking all possible precautions, brought the panelled glass panes to New York and finally to France. It is very slightly painted, only a sketch, but enchanting. I have it in my writing room.

Maugham was swamped with ideas and with exhilaration. He was often travelling under harsh conditions, but he listened to the riff-raff with no less eagerness than he had to the great Lillie Langtry. She had told him neat stories, but these people were artless enough to enact theirs. Celebrities never interested him as much as the rough and the smooth of a steamship's passenger list. Celebrities guarded their myths and their tongues; the South Seas and its inhabitants were innocent of such caution. They were like the lady missionary's girls who knew no shame. Maugham gathered the fruit with both hands. Haxton was invaluable, for he had the gift of the gab. But it was Maugham whose eavesdropping ear caught the nuances and measured the silences. 'I stepped off my pedestal,' he said later, with a certain ambiguity. He also put his spying skills to useful purpose. On this occasion he certainly got the goods.

One cannot altogether be surprised that the return to civilization and to Syrie was something of an anticlimax. It must be accounted a sober fact that he now recognized himself as a homosexual. The old persona was sloughed forever. The unsatisfactory element in *Of Human Bondage* was, on his own confession, the ending. Did he now know why? He was not the kind of person whose problems were resoluble by marriage, or by General Practice; he might lash Syrie for her supposed frailties (and he did not stop short of accusing her openly of rank fraud) but the fault lay less with her than with him. Fault? It was a flaw in him, at least in the geographic sense, his homosexuality, for it tilted the landscape of his mind and yet remained unacknowledged, like the fault that runs through San Francisco and renders that elegant city so dangerous for its inhabitants that they never speak of it.

Of Human Bondage had been published in August 1915. In it he had portrayed a hero broken by fate and healed, in the end, by love and by a sense of purpose. It has a

The Gauguin painting on glass that Maugham acquired in Tahiti.

strength and a fullness he was never again to match. He became smoother and more poised. His prose lost its ponderous sincerity; it grew light and elastic but it was never again at the service of a man who was seeking to find his own integrity. It became a screen so cleverly illuminated with figures that the public took them for real. *Of Human Bondage* had no immediate success. Wartime London preferred Gaiety girls to sensitive anguish. In New York things were different, thanks largely to a review by Theodore Dreiser, an earnest thunderer in the cause of naturalism and himself a Zola-esque writer of constipated power, author of *Sister Carrie* and *An American Tragedy*.

One feels as though one were sitting before a splendid Shiraz or Daghestan of priceless texture or intricate weave, admiring, feeling, responding sensually to its colours or tones. Or better yet, it is as though a symphony of great beauty by a master, Strauss or Beethoven, had just been completed, and the bud notes and flower tones were filling the air with their elusive message, fluttering and dying.

It is not easy to imagine such a notice causing people to pelt the booksellers with *louis d'or*, or with dollars, but Dreiser's comparison of the author with Jesus ('we may actually walk and talk with one whose hands and feet have been pierced with nails') may have turned the trick. At all events, the novel sold well and Maugham's reputation as a novelist was decisively re-established. (It is pertinent to note that *Of Human Bondage* was more enthusiastically received in America, where his fame and riches as a playwright earned him less envy in literary circles.)

Soon after his marriage Maugham was again recruited into the Secret Service. The head of British Intelligence in New York was Sir William Wiseman, an old friend of Maugham's family. Wiseman asked him to go to Russia, where the internal situation was already deteriorating; the British Government was afraid that Russia might make a separate peace, especially if the Bolsheviks obtained supreme power. His mission was to bolster the Russian war effort by assisting the Provisional Government of Alexander Kerensky to stay in command. To this end, Maugham was supplied with a quantity of Allied gold substantial enough to enable the Government to buy arms and to finance newspapers in support of their plans. Four Czechs travelled with Maugham (though they affected not to know each other) in order to act as a liaison between him and Jan Masaryk, the leader of 60,000 Czechs who were determined to stay in the war and create a separate Czecho-Slovak state when it was won.

Maugham led what seems a curious life in the war. At times he was deeply involved and then he was off on his private affairs. Dour patriots might accuse him of a certain dilettantism, but he was, by the standards of the day, too old to fight and he certainly cannot be accused of recalcitrance. He had contracted an infection of the lungs in Switzerland and had a haemorrhage in New York shortly before his arduous journey to St Petersburg. He could honourably have escaped his mission. He told Wiseman that he did not consider himself competent, but Sir William assured him that it had been decided that he would do as well as anyone else. He went.

In St Petersburg, the British Embassy authorities, instructed to allow him to send his messages under their auspices but through a code unknown to them, greeted him with ostentatious frigidity. War was one thing, manners another, and no war could excuse a breach of propriety like expecting people to forward messages without

Alexander Kerensky (second from the right) in the Kremlin, 1917.

The Gauguin still-life that Maugham saw in Norway.

knowing what they were. Maugham was able to retrieve his unhappy position by acting as intermediary between the American Ambassador, a chap called Francis, and the British Ambassador, Sir George Buchanan, who had inadvertently offended his colleague by an excess of English reserve. After the two Allies had been reconciled, the British Embassy transmitted his telegrams with less surliness, but neither Maugham's gold nor Kerensky's eloquence could sustain the Russian war effort.

For all its absurdities, Maugham took his Intelligence work seriously enough. He believed that had he arrived six months earlier he might have prevented the triumph of the Bolsheviks; as it was, he saw that the inevitable could not be avoided. He analysed the character of Kerensky with admirable clarity (in *A Writer's Notebook*) and his telegrams were plainly blunt in their estimate of Russia's will to fight. He left St Petersburg a few weeks before the Bolsheviks' seizure of power and took a personal message from Kerensky to Lloyd George. It was a passionate, well-argued plea for help and understanding. Maugham, fearing that his stammer would prevent him from delivering it with the fervour of which Kerensky was such a master, wrote it down. He travelled home by way of Norway where he happened to see, in the gallery at Christiania, a painting of some tropical fruit by Gauguin. It was fate's reminder to him that, once the world's game was played, he had a novel to finish.

He went to Downing Street for a meeting with Lloyd George (Kerensky had called him Llord George) and found the Prime Minister extremely charming. He

49

was a great admirer of Maugham's plays and he spoke at length and with amiable temper of the world situation. It was only when Maugham proffered Kerensky's *cri de cœur* that a blight fell on the conversation. Lloyd George could not or would not meet the Russian's demands. What was Maugham to tell Kerensky? 'Just that I can't do it,' Lloyd George repeated. Maugham returned to his hotel. He was ill and he was worried. His worries were soon and abruptly dispelled. The Bolsheviks seized power and Lloyd George's impotence or unwillingness was never reported. Nor did Maugham return to Russia. His illness was diagnosed as tuberculosis. He was asked by Rufus Isaacs, the Lord Chief Justice, to go to Romania on another secret mission. Although he was willing again to risk his health in the British cause, the news of his condition led Isaacs to insist that he look after his lungs and leave Romania to other hands. He entered Banchory Sanatorium in Kincardine, near Aberdeen, for three months' complete rest.

Boredom did not damp his spirits; he read (Russia had renewed his interest in Dostoyevsky) and he wrote a new play, *Home and Beauty*, perhaps the most perfect of all his comedies, and, as always, he made notes. His condition soon improved, for after a few months he was able to join Syrie and their child at Charles Hill Court, a rented house near Frensham in Surrey. They were near Highmead, where the novelist Robert Hichens lived with his family, and there was much happy socializing; they played croquet and they rode in the Surrey countryside. All the while Maugham wrote steadily; another play, *Caesar's Wife*, and *The Moon and Sixpence* occupied his mornings. (He wrote his plays with professional efficiency: one week for each act and a final week to polish.)

One day, when he was out riding, he was badly thrown. Hichens reports his reaction:

. . . we were trotting quietly along the high-road deep in an interesting conversation, when the roan suddenly crashed on to the road, inevitably throwing his rider. Maugham's forehead struck the road and blood came. It was a really dangerous fall. . . . I forget what we did, but I know that we both sat for some minutes by the side of the road, waiting till Maugham, who had been nearly stunned, recovered enough to remount. He behaved like a stoic, made no complaint, and presently said he was ready to get on the animal which had treated him so badly, and which he was holding by the reins.

Alec Waugh remarks of this period, one of great productiveness (he was also working on a volume of stories, *The Trembling of a Leaf*, and on the *Ashenden* cycle), that he was 'passing through a series of harrowing domestic crises'. If so, he must have carried them off with no less stoicism than his fall from the horse. Maugham says that he and his wife lived 'amicably' together. She was keen to return to London life. Maugham had to go back to the sanatorium in the late autumn, after having been in town for the last air raids of the war. While Willie was in Scotland, Syrie supervised the decoration of their new house in Wyndham Place. Osbert Sitwell remembered with impressed gratitude the elegance of the entertaining which took place in the 'large, beige-painted, barrel-vaulted drawing room' of the Maughams' house. Syrie's talent for interior decoration was to bring her international success and at this time she opened her first antique shop. She was the originator of the white rooms which were so chic in the eyes of those who did not have to clean them.

Opposite, Maugham's wife, Syrie; they were married in 1916 and divorced in 1927.

A Gauguin painting, *Contes barbares*, that illustrates the theme of *The Moon and Sixpence*, based on Gauguin's life.

Opposite, Gerald Haxton, Maugham's companion and secretary until his death in 1944.

The Maughams did not divorce until 1927 (the same year in which Frederick Maugham became a High Court judge), but it would be an excess of caution not to suppose that the breakdown of the marriage was due almost entirely to Willie's inability to forget Gerald Haxton.

Maugham was back in London for the season in 1919. In the summer he and Syrie rented Alfred Sutro's house near Hambledon. *The Moon and Sixpence* was published and seemed to confirm his reputation as a serious novelist. Maxwell Anderson, one of the new lions of American writing, praised it highly. Desmond MacCarthy, whom Maugham had met in Flanders, was now an eager and influential advocate in England. Maugham somewhat resented MacCarthy's use of a private conversation, in which Maugham had adverted to certain of his own possible weaknesses as a writer, but there can be no question that MacCarthy was a genuine admirer, though his study, *The English Maupassant*, did not appear until 1933. Maugham seemed on the way to that unquestioned literary eminence which his theatrical career had impeded.

The Moon and Sixpence introduced the character of Ashenden, who was to serve as his persona until the end of the *entre deux guerres*. The main character, Charles Strickland, is an English stockbroker who deserts his wife and children in order to become a painter and proves impervious to Ashenden's conventional reproaches concerning his responsibilities and morals. He goes to the South Seas, takes a Polynesian mistress and dies of leprosy in a native hut. Strickland is a good deal less complex than Gauguin and a good deal more romantic a character. He is the sort of painter whom John Berger finds so obstreperous in fiction, a strutting genius whose art is all to do with passion and innate flair. He is too good and too bad to be true. The strength of the story lies less in its analysis of a painter's psychology (for Maugham was always hesitant in assuming knowledge of what lay beyond his observant competence) than in its portrait of a man severing the bonds of the commonplace and daring to find his own society sufficient unto itself. Philip Carey, lacking the gift, was obliged to make his peace with society; Strickland, the artist, has the means and the will (shades of Schopenhauer here?) to kiss Europe good-bye and follow his demon to hell and beyond. It is this triumph of nerve which makes Strickland so powerful and memorable a hero. It is significant, perhaps, that it was at this point in his fiction that Maugham distanced himself from the boldness he so clearly admired; if the ghost of the author figures in *The Moon and Sixpence*, it is in the person of the buttoned Ashenden, not the audacious Strickland. So far as society is concerned, Maugham himself remained eager to wound, but afraid to strike.

The East called strongly to him. By the end of 1919 he was again on his way to the South Seas. He went by way of Chicago, which was to be the home town of Edward Barnard, seduced by the irresponsible ways of Polynesia, in the story 'The Fall of Edward Barnard', and of Larry Darrell in *The Razor's Edge*. It was also where he again met up with Gerald Haxton. While in Chicago he visited the slaughter-houses and he read Sinclair Lewis's new novel, *Main Street*. For the first time he felt that the Midwesterners in the railroad club car were understandable and accessible to him. Sinclair Lewis's father was a doctor and Lewis's style had something of Maugham's own clinical clarity and accurate ear. Maugham detected in *Main Street* the beginnings of a class consciousness he had taken to be absent from transatlantic life.

For someone who had visited Henry James in New England (in 1910), it is surprising that he should have required Lewis to alert him to the stratification of American society.

Gerald Haxton now became Maugham's official secretary. He was an invaluable companion, as the dedication of *A Writer's Notebook* makes plain: 'In Loving Memory of My Friend, Frederick Gerald Haxton'. He was gregarious and he was charming. He was able to introduce himself into all kinds of company. He enjoyed Willie's money, but he might be said to have given good value for it. Apart from typing manuscripts, he had an ear for scandal and he was wise to scoundrels. He was as quick-witted as Maugham was stammering. He knew his way about. They went to China, to the Federated Malay States and to Indo-China. British colonial society gave them a ready welcome; in the monotonous life of rubber-planting and petty administration, a celebrity whose theatrical successes were advertised in the out-of-date issues of *The Times* that came on the steamers was a bright spark indeed. If there was ennui in this expatriate society that dreamed of the reward of home leave as saints did of paradise, there were also high spirits and high jinks; Maugham was later excoriated for abusing the hospitality of those whom he depicted with such recognizable clarity but he could scarcely be accused of having misrepresented them. An official's memoirs gives evidence that colonial life was fraught with 'Maughamian' dramas:

There was, for example, the famous incident in which the Resident Councillor of X, having retired for his Sunday siesta, suddenly awoke with suspicions in his mind, and hieing himself to his wife's room, found her in bed with a member of the Legislative Council who had been a guest at their curry tiffin. The Member of Council dropped deftly over the verandah on to the gravel and was pursued round and round the Residency – the Member in his shirt and the Resident Councillor in his pyjamas. And each time the Resident Councillor passed the Sikh sentry on duty, the latter presented arms!

Maugham's globe-trotting during the twenties was such that he seems, at times, to have been all but ubiquitous. He was in China in 1920, but he was also in London, late in the year, for the production of his play, *The Unknown*, in which appeared both his favourite actor, C. V. France, and Haidée Wright, whose performance he rated as the most moving he had ever seen. In 1921, *The Circle* was produced; his volume of stories, *The Trembling of a Leaf*, came out in the same year. Among them were 'Rain' and 'The Fall of Edward Barnard' whose heroine was to be revamped for *The Razor's Edge* some twenty years later. *East of Suez* was produced in 1922 and the travel book *On a Chinese Screen* was the prompt result of his visit to China. *East of Suez* was a spectacular drama which enabled him to escape from smart drawing-rooms into the bazaars and alleys of the Orient. Eugene Goossens was commissioned to write the music for a mime sequence and, having no idea what Chinese music sounded like, had to track down an amateur orchestra of Chinese working men in a Soho back street.

In the same year Maugham was back in the South Seas once again. He and Haxton visited Borneo, where they narrowly escaped drowning. While travelling up the Sarawak River in a boat with a crew of convicts, they were overtaken by a tidal bore. The boat capsized and everyone was thrown into the water. The boat kept

Opposite, Maugham's Far East; a view of the Malacca waterfront, in the Malay States.

revolving under the force of the waves and Maugham felt his strength going. Only Haxton's encouragement and the lucky chance which enabled them to make a lifebelt of one of the light mattresses that furnished the boat saved Maugham's life. He was exhausted but the two of them, with a couple of the crew, were able to strike out for the shore. They just made it, trekking the last heavy steps through thick mud. Maugham had scarcely recovered before Haxton had a heart attack. It seemed that he would die, but there was nothing to do but keep him quiet and hope for the best. At last the other white man in the boat came along in a canoe and rescued them. They spent the night in a Dyak long-house. The incident furnished Maugham with the idea for 'The Yellow Streak', in which a man betrays his companion and, ignoring his cries for help when the boat capsizes, saves himself, only to find, with horror, that the other man has also survived. The coward has native blood in his veins and his inferiority complex feeds his paranoia. In fact, it turns out that his fellow passenger has no notion that he had been abandoned, but by then it is too late. There is no evidence that Maugham himself had any such yellow streak (or any but the best bourgeois blood), but the possibility of such treachery must have gone through his mind and the way in which the incident was converted into an ironic tale is a good example of his alert, unfanciful imagination.

It was at this time that he wrote his only children's story, 'The Princess September and the Nightingale'. It is set in Siam and has a pleasing tartness in its moral which makes it very much part of the *œuvre*, for all its light-heartedness. It was published in *Pearson's Magazine* and in the New York edition of *Good Housekeeping*. (Later it appeared in the volume *The Gentleman in the Parlour*.) In a caption, the editor of *Pearson's Magazine* stated that 'this delightful story was written by Mr Maugham for a very special purpose, the nature of which we are not, at the moment, permitted to disclose'. The special purpose was that the story was included in the miniature manuscript library of the Queen's Doll's House. The library contains 200 volumes written in their authors' own hands. Maugham's measures $3.5 \times 3 \times 1.2$ centimetres; there are fifty-three leaves of miniature manuscript, a considerable effort of calligraphy. Maugham may have found the work less arduous than would a modern writer; he never typed, even when he wrote a film-script. It is somewhat ironic, however, that he should have taken such humble pains over a royal command of this kind while spending all of his time with Haxton and engaged in a liaison of a kind which the King, George V, found so incomprehensible that he once said, 'I thought men like that shot themselves.'

In the twenties, men like that preferred to go and live in the South of France. Those who lacked the means were obliged, of course, to run the gauntlet of blackmail and fear which humbug, hypocrisy and the conventional morality did not fail to engender. There were others who took refuge in a colourful, even outrageous eccentricity, and Maugham no doubt had met many of them in the theatre, to which he continued to contribute a flow of successful comedies and dramas. There was no question of challenging the prevailing *mores* or of changing his own manner. Who can doubt that the aloofness which had once concealed his shyness now served to hide his homosexuality? In London he was always alone. Haxton stayed on the Continent.

The theatre did not fail to provide Maugham with a large income and a public platform, but it was a platform on which he was obliged to say agreeable things. Even

so commercial a playwright, who had made plenty of managers plenty of money, was not always able to find backing for his plays. There was none for *The Road Uphill*, which once more dealt with the desire to break away from the crushing banalities of bourgeois family life and which furnished him, eventually, with the basis for *The Razor's Edge*. When *The Sacred Flame* was produced in New York, it was a flop. Seriousness was not a saleable commodity in the post-war world.

The theme of *The Sacred Flame* had been suggested to him by the devotion of his sister-in-law, Charles's wife, to one of her children who had suffered a terrible accident. In the play, Maugham makes the child a wounded war veteran whose mother, realizing the futility of his agony, lovingly assists him to die. Suicide was a device he used frequently in his early novels and death is something which, time and again, he tried to deal with in a casual, or at least natural way, without excessive dramatics or lamentations. He seems always to have been very conscious of it. The medical student had, of course, to become used to corpses and to blood and Maugham lacked the squeamishness of a comfortable society which, even after a murderous war, still managed not to notice reality. He had, his manner always suggests, seen a thing or two. Nor was he above rubbing his audience's nose in the mud; fine sentiments disgusted him, for he was always aware of the biological limitations of the human condition. Would he not have been a different man had someone known how to alter the shape of his jaw when he was young by the simple use of a gold band? What if he had not stammered? Or if he had been six feet tall, instead of five feet seven?

The twenties were a period of increased fame and popularity, yet he was not popular for his serious opinions but as that Somerset Maugham who gave the West End 'typical' plays like *The Circle* and *Caesar's Wife*, in which he so admired Fay Compton, and *Our Betters*, which made a sensation in 1923, the same year as *Home and Beauty*. The gossips had it that a character in *Our Betters* was founded on Gordon Selfridge, the American department store magnate, and as so often, the gossips had it right. Selfridge, it was disclosed in *Looking Back*, had once been madly in love with Syrie and had offered to settle £5,000 a year on her. She refused. The play was written in 1915, in Italy, and Maugham was amused that the critics, who did not know how early it came in his *œuvre*, detected in it the development of themes present in plays that had in fact been written after it. Nothing gave him such quiet pleasure as laughing up his sleeve at a critic.

In 1923 Maugham visited Ceylon and Burma. He travelled without fuss and with great vigilance. Most of the British carried their Britishness with them like an ostentatious piece of luggage. They refused, as a matter almost of conscience, to touch the natives with a bargepole (although, of course, there was always a surreptitious and sometimes a flagrant sexual use to be made of them) and Maugham's sense of the superficiality and the cruelty of the complacent planters and officials was enlarged by their pettiness and their unbounded and unwarranted contempt for the world around them which Maugham found so absorbing and so liberating. There is no doubt that in his estimation the main burden in the East was the White Man.

There is a large gap in *A Writer's Notebook* between 1923 and 1929. No doubt Maugham continued to take notes during those years, but the lacuna argues a period of anguish and unhappy memories.

He later claimed that Syrie had lovers and that they were pretty worthless. On the other hand, he had Gerald Haxton. In London he might play the aggrieved husband, but the grievances were never all his. Syrie was now a successful decorator with clients on both sides of the Atlantic. They were together when they were together (often at parties where Maugham found the raffish company little to his taste) and when they were apart, they were often very far apart indeed. Publicly, however, success followed success. The fruits of the East ripened and went to market and were prodigiously appetizing to their audience.

He continued to travel widely. In 1924 he went to Mexico, where he attended a luncheon at which Frieda and D. H. Lawrence were present. The two men did not take to each other. Frieda's attitude was less hostile than her husband's. She wrote, 'I felt sorry for Maugham. He seemed to me an unhappy and acid man who got no fun out of living . . . he could not accept the narrow social world and yet he did not

Still from the film of *Our Betters* (with Constance Bennett), made in 1933.

believe in a wider human one. . . . When I met other writers then I knew without knowing how altogether different Lawrence was. They may have been good writers, but Lawrence was a genius.' Lawrence himself observed in a letter to Curtis Brown, '[Maugham] hates it here [Mexico City]: has gone to Yucatan. He'll hate it there. I didn't like him.' He did not like Maugham's work either and later wrote with dismissive acuity of the shortcomings of *Ashenden*, which he reviewed when it came out.

In 1925 came a new full-length novel, *The Painted Veil*. It is the only one of his novels in which the plot preceded the characters. It is a melodrama of colonial life with a heroine who has some of the calamitous characteristics of Emma Bovary. The setting was originally Hong Kong, but the Assistant Secretary of the Hong Kong Government protested and the place-names were all changed. Hong Kong became Tching-Yen, and so forth. The book had already been printed when the scandal broke and a few smart reviewers, who already had their copies, were less than scrupulous about returning the withdrawn edition. A libel action concerning the names of the principal couple had to be settled out of court, for £250; their name was

The PAINTED VEIL
W SOMERSET MAUGHAM

then changed from Lane to Fane, which suggests that the legal action was opportunist rather than founded on a genuine grievance. Maugham would surely have changed it to a totally different name had not the parties been easily satisfied by their damages.

The plot is simple and dramatic, perhaps too dramatic and too simple for the serious fictional reputation which Maugham appeared to have consolidated with *The Moon and Sixpence*. Walter Fane's wife is unfaithful to him with a colonial Casanova, Charlie Townsend, who is himself married to a dowdy woman. When Fane finds out, he takes his wife on a dangerous mission to an area in mainland China where cholera is raging. He catches the disease to which he had deliberately exposed his wife and 'the dog it was that died'. The widow returns to Tching-Yen, imagining that Charlie will now leave his wife and marry her. But Charlie is in no mind to do any such thing; sex is one thing, marriage another. Kitty returns to England a sadder and wiser woman. Her wisdom is the fruit not only of her rejection by Townsend but also of her encounter, in the cholera district, with an alcoholic expatriate doctor who serves, as doctors often do, to convey to her the wry resignation which is the happiest recipe Maugham can offer to those sentenced to the human condition.

The Painted Veil did not fail to please the public, but it was a piece of professionalism with no claim to originality or profundity. The very skill with which it is turned amounts almost to cynicism in its least amiable form, contempt for the reader. This may be due less to calculation than to the abstract way in which the *donnée* first presented itself, but serious critics could be excused, on this occasion, for regarding Maugham as a figure of no substantial interest. Compared to Kipling or to E. M. Forster, whose *A Passage to India* was published in the previous year,

Opposite, dust-jacket of the first edition of *The Painted Veil.*

Maugham seems pedestrian and even perfunctory. The short stories contained in *The Casuarina Tree* (1926) were, on the other hand, among his best; they included 'The Yellow Streak', 'The Letter' (a success later as a play and a film), 'Before the Party' and 'The Outstation'. Nearly all of these are substantial *contes*, in the manner of Maupassant, and lack the blandness to be found in *The Painted Veil* (which was also filmed, with Greta Garbo). 'The Letter' was so scandalously *à clef* as to amount to a flagrant breach of hospitality and perhaps of good taste.

Maugham was not happy with his American publishers' promotion of *The Painted Veil*, and accused them of sending it out 'like a parcel of tea'. His letter of complaint insists that he is concerned with seeking 'distinction rather than lucre', which makes it all the more strange that he should have sought it with so undistinguished a book. However, for all his irritation, he remained with Doran (who were later to be bought out by Doubleday) and his fidelity to his publishers on both sides of the Atlantic, as elsewhere, remained unruptured.

In 1926 *The Constant Wife*, an amusing though perhaps slightly laborious comedy of changing sexual manners, was given its first production. The leading part was taken in America by Ethel Barrymore. The first night was a fiasco. Miss Barrymore fluffed her lines, intruded speeches from other plays and performed sections of the third act during the first. Garson Kanin, the playwright and screen-writer, tells the story as he had it from Maugham's account:

He went back to see her afterwards in a fury. As he walked into her dressing room, she said, 'Oh darling, I've ruined your beautiful play, but it'll run a year.' Maugham then says, 'She had and it did.' It was one of his few set-piece stories. I have heard him tell it seven or eight times, and always word for word the same. (In 1949 on a broadcast celebrating Ethel's seventieth birthday, Maugham, in his part of it, said quite plainly that during rehearsals he had fallen madly in love with her.)

His homosexuality was never the whole explanation of his personality nor did it preclude heterosexual desire. He was sometimes accused of misogyny and it is true that his women can behave with alarming vanity and greed, but some of them also have a sturdy resilience and an eye for falseness which their creator did not think the least of virtues. Constance, who was played by Ingrid Bergman in the London revival of 1973, shows admirable resource and coolness in coping with an errant husband and contrives a pretty revenge with a lack of rancour in a way that seems, it must be said, more an idealization than a criticism of women. Such constancy demands affection rather than love, tolerance rather than desire. Was Constance Maugham's ideal wife? If we are to believe the shrill evidence of Beverley Nichols's catchpenny memoir, *A Case of Human Bondage*, published hard on Maugham's death by the same publisher to whom he had been faithful for sixty years, his own wife's fault was not so much her worldliness as her jealous devotion. Be that as it may, in 1927 Syrie abandoned all hope of recapturing her husband's love and they were divorced. Maugham often ruefully declared that he lacked poetic genius. The bold flight was not for him. It is, therefore, perhaps significant that in the Notebook under the date 1927 there appears a section of verse entitled simply 'Lines' which at once celebrate and lament a love-affair in which a man attempts always to get away but about whom the woman always 'throws her soft arms' and whom she always

Dust-jacket design of *The Casuarina Tree*, a collection of short stories published in 1926.

The writer Beverley Nichols, who was a long-time friend of Maugham's.

recaptures. It seems to be a confession of weakness and an accusation of possessiveness, but the spell that the woman casts is strong and its strength is acknowledged. What passed between Maugham and Syrie was a transaction of more subtlety than any superficial judgment could perceive.

There have been, quite properly, many defences of Syrie, whose affection for Willie endured all his enmity (she was a keen advocate of *The Razor's Edge* when it was published in 1944), and probably her only fault was that he had ceased to love her. Perhaps her passionate feminity served to confirm to him that he was indeed 'three quarters queer' and agreeable though he may have found Haxton (and the boys they encountered in the East), it was probably a piece of self-knowledge that he could have done without. The long shadow of Oscar Wilde lay across his life. Though he was to entertain many homosexuals at the Villa Mauresque, which he bought in 1928, he never made any suggestion, however impersonal, that the brutal English laws against homosexual practices should be repealed or altered. Reformers solicited his help in vain. He had attended a dinner, during the days of Wilde's disgrace, in obstinate honour of the most scintillating wit of his time, but he never broke his silence over the love that dared not speak its name.

Opposite, a painting by Gerald Kelly of Maugham at work in the late 1920s.

The Villa Mauresque on Cap Ferrat, where Maugham was to live for the rest of his life, apart from the war years, was not the most beautiful villa on the coast, though it was in one of the most beautiful parts of it. Cap Ferrat is a narrow peninsula jutting into the Mediterranean between Nice and Monte Carlo; it is at once isolated and convenient to the Riviera where the casinos appealed so keenly to Gerald Haxton. Cap Ferrat had once belonged to Leopold II, King of the Belgians. He built on it a palatial residence for himself and three houses for his three mistresses. He was as superstitious as he was sensual and dreaded the risk of dying before he had received the Sacrament of Extreme Unction. He therefore engaged an elderly ecclesiastic to whom he gave a stretch of land and a grant to build a house near enough to his own so that His Majesty could make his peace with God before he died. The Bishop had spent most of his life in Algeria and he built himself a Moorish house. Maugham was to call it the Villa Mauresque, although he did not move into it until the more elaborate of the retired Bishop's excrescences had been removed from what then turned out to be a plain, if ample, residence. There were twenty acres of grounds. The price was of the order of £16,000; later Maugham was to estimate that the place was worth over $2,000,000. Of course, he had done a few things to it. In his writing-room he installed the glass panels from the door which Gauguin had painted in Tahiti and on the gatepost of his Moorish house he incised (and painted in burnt sienna) the device which graced his books and which his father had brought back from the Mahgreb.

The entrance to the Villa Mauresque, showing the Moorish symbol which also adorned Maugham's printed works.

Guests and friends included the Windsors (*right*), the eccentric expatriate American Romaine Brooks (*below*), the Duff Coopers (*opposite right*), H. G. Wells (see his Christmas 1934 dedication of one of his books 'To Willie, God bless him', *opposite below*).

Through those gates were to come celebrities of all kinds, both social and literary. They included kings (of Sweden and Siam) and ex-kings (the Duke of Windsor), the ex-Queen of Spain, the Maharanee of Baroda, the Aga Khan and his wife, Winston Churchill and Lord Beaverbrook. Of authors there were all sorts: Glenway Westcott, S. J. Perelman, Moss Hart, H. G. Wells (who was a neighbour), Arnold Bennett (whose steam-yacht was convenient for Mediterranean calls – he too had come a long way from Le Chat Blanc) and J. B. Priestley, Kipling and Coward and Arlen, the whole fashionable *galère*. There was tennis and there was swimming. There were handsome young men for those who liked handsome young men and there was bridge for those who liked bridge. There was excellent food – Maugham was said to have, in his Annette, the best cook in private service in France – and there was a sort of attention which few country-houses could boast any longer: a valet and a maid for each guest, carefully chosen books and beautiful flowers. For a Stoic, Maugham made an excellent Epicurus. Twenty years before, he had wondered how much he should, or could, tip his hostesses' servants. That problem was not likely to exercise the smart people whom he entertained at the Villa Mauresque. He was a generous host and a considerate employer. He made it a rule that his servants should eat the same meals as his guests; he trained them with care and treated them with tact. They stayed. Even a butler who 'really would not do' stayed for twenty-five years. (As an act of petty spite, he destroyed Maugham's address-book when he did finally leave.) But if his guests had the impression that they had entered a carefully administered Eden, where there was nothing but luxury and where their host proved the most amiable of serpents, they were mistaken. They might themselves do nothing during their maximum of a fortnight's stay (like his work, Maugham's invitations had clearly defined beginnings and ends) but their host was not idle. He worked every morning in the severely furnished study where the view over the sea towards Nice was blocked up because the Master was there to work, not to daydream. He sat at a substantial eight-foot table, rather lower than the standard work-table. Mr Maugham had become a man of substance, but he was well aware that he had not added a cubit to his stature.

The twenties were a period not only of lavish living, at least for some, and of escapist entertainment, of musical comedy and champagne; they were also a period of literary innovation and creative fervour. Before the war, Maugham had not failed (if Ashenden is any witness) to be impressed by the *Ballets Russes* and the revival of interest in ikons and in Russian writing which came in the wake of Diaghilev and Nijinsky, but the influence of the Americans, like Pound and Eliot, Scott Fitzgerald and Hemingway, who did so much to change the attitudes and the style of a new generation of writers, was largely lost on him. He admired Hemingway and Sinclair Lewis and he was always to enjoy the company of Americans, especially those like S. N. Behrman, whose sharp New York wit made him laugh.

But for all that he had learnt from Sinclair Lewis about Middle America and for all his success on the New York stage and for all his love of American cocktails (the Manhattan and the Dry Martini especially) and of Gerald Haxton, who made them to perfection, Maugham was decidedly a European writer. Dr Johnson accused David Hume of writing French and Maugham is open to the same accusation. He imagined that he always wrote simply, but he was prone to curious little pedantries and to sentences which, if not elaborate, came out in an order which appears idiosyncratic, even perverse, until one realizes that the ghost of a French usage or a French word order lingers behind the mannered simplicities. The influence of Balzac and of Maupassant was not easily uprooted. Why should it have been? They remain two of the freshest and the most inventive of writers. *Le Père Goriot* was one of Maugham's favourite novels; *Le Rouge et le Noir* was another, for who could not wish to emulate Stendhal's passionate precision? *Of Human Bondage* is included in Cyril Connolly's list of a hundred books of the modern movement, but if Maugham had been in at the beginning, he lost touch with the *avant-garde* as it charged through the twenties, trailing shocks and sparks. Despite Eliot's insistence on 'the objective correlative', the new generation were more concerned with art than with life; they exploded the old forms and they heaped scorn on conventional expectations.

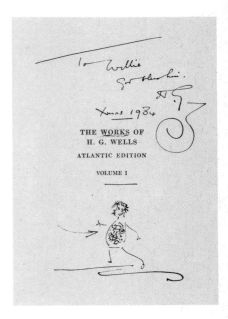

In all of this, Maugham had little part. His post-war plays reflected a changed society, in which divorce untied marriages and tied up plots with a facility that would have been unthinkable and implausible in the Edwardian era, but they did not reflect any change in theatrical ideas as such. They had beginnings, middles and ends. All the great actresses appeared in his work: Marie Tempest, Fay Compton, Marie Löhr, Gladys Cooper. Maugham always offered them excellent opportunities for doing the things they did best, but he preferred to abandon the theatre rather than to alter it. He soldiered on (in the highest ranks) until 1933, but success had become, as it often does, a source of inhibition rather than a warrant for boldness. He disliked the conventions, but he expressed his dislike conventionally.

Maugham posed beside the pool at Villa
Mauresque – setting for his introduction
to the film *Encore*, made in 1951.

The route to France; a Channel Ferry
poster by Cassandre, 1931.

His absence from England meant that he lost touch with the new. However sedulously the exile reads the papers, however shrewdly he pumps his guests, there seems to be a law which says that a man is frozen, so far as his native culture is concerned, at the moment when he leaves his native shores. His vocabulary becomes dated (till the end of his life Maugham spoke of 'the omnibus') and his social attitudes rigidify.

Though Maugham was a sardonic enemy of prudishness, he was shocked when he heard, in the 1950s, of a certain American performer who, while staying at the Dorchester Hotel, brought back young men from the Edgware Road and enjoyed them in his suite. It was not that such things were not done (there was no shortage of sailors at the Mauresque), but that they were not done at the Dorchester. Maugham quit England when he was in his early fifties. Though he continued to travel with enormous energy and appetite, he paid the price for his decision. He was marooned among the comfortable and the pretty. He did not deliberately sever himself from the young or the indigent; if they came to him, he could treat them with charm and without condescension, but he no longer had the regular opportunity to, so to say, bump into them. His travels were, no doubt, a way of re-immersing himself in the fortuitous no less than the picturesque (in 1929 he was again in Borneo), but they were no substitute for belonging to a society; the price of distancing himself from reality was, even for so wide-ranging a voyager, a contraction of his world. He had emigrated not only to France but, as the rich often do, to the past. He remained an Edwardian, for all his cocktails and for all the nude bathing at the Villa Mauresque. He did not take part in the literary twenties because, quite simply, he was not there at the time. However, it may well be that his mannered realism is as good a passport to the ages as any of the experimental brilliances of novelists who seemed, at the time, more significant than he.

Ashenden was published in 1928 and though it has had a not inconsiderable influence on its *genre*, there is nothing in it to suggest that its author was once the admirer of James Joyce, nothing to suggest that new ways of telling stories, new ideas of what a story was, were current. D. H. Lawrence reviewed the volume in *Vogue* on 20 July 1928. His comments were mercilessly perspicuous, and perhaps better than any other piece of critical writing they reveal why it is that Maugham failed to reach the highest standards:

If, on the other hand, you get a decent, straight individual, especially an individual capable of feeling love for another, then you are made to see that such a person is a despicable fool, encompassing his own destruction. So the American dies for his dirty washing, the Hindu dies for a blowsy woman who wants her wrist-watch back, the Greek merchant is murdered by mistake, and so on. It is better to be a live dirty dog than a dead lion, says Mr Ashenden. Perhaps it is, to Mr Ashenden. But these stories, being 'serious', are faked. Mr Maugham is a splendid observer. He can bring before us persons and places most excellently. But as soon as the excellently observed characters have to move, it is a fake. Mr Maugham gives them a humorous shove or two. We find they are nothing but puppets, instruments of the author's pet prejudice. The author's pet prejudice being 'humour', it would be hard to find a bunch of more ill-humoured stories, in which the humour has gone more rancid.

Ashenden's originality lay in the low-key realism with which it examined the treachery and double-dealing not of smart marriage but of international espionage. Willie Ashenden, with whom the author so closely identified himself that he would sometimes introduce himself under that name in real life, is never personally in danger and so avoids affectations of heroic coolness or intrepid initiative. He is rather a cold fish, commissioning murder (in 'The Hairless Mexican') or contriving the execution of a double agent (in 'The Traitor'), whose technical treason does not prevent him from being a more affectionate and more deeply loved man than the narrator. Maugham deliberately presents his *alter ego* in a sour light. This device, which he used so often in order to heighten the effect of his story – himself remaining dry-eyed, in Desmond MacCarthy's estimation, the better to prompt our tears – and in order to keep his prose free of cloying sentiment, was so effective that in the end he was accused of being incapable of human feeling or human pity. It is unlikely that this is a fair charge. His medical training, no less than his temperament, had taught him that one cannot diagnose accurately through a haze of sentiment and that the best analysis of a condition is achieved by those who have the nerve to swab aside the blood and look calmly at the wound.

Ashenden is said by Robert Calder, in his excellent *W. Somerset Maugham and the Quest for Freedom*, to be of a piece with much of the debunking literature about the Great War which had begun to appear in the late twenties, but if the suggestion is that Maugham was following a fashion, it is a little harsh. The view of motives and the taste for irony are scarcely changed from *The Hero*. It is a common criticism of Maugham that he gave the public what they wanted, but most of the themes which seem suspiciously fashionable are ones which interested him long before the fashions came. He may have been led to write about them at periods which seemed propitious, but his interest was not itself cynically concocted. *Ashenden* certainly strikes no bellicose patriotic attitudes (it observes the flukes and cruelties of the Great War with much the same attitude as Maupassant did those of 1870) but the narrator is far from indifferent. Indeed the heartlessness of his boss, R., the forerunner of James Bond's M., obviously somewhat scandalizes Ashenden, not least because it so lacks the idealism which the worldly, yet naïve, Willie would like to associate with his own side. In fact, Maugham felt a fool on discovering that he alone, of the Geneva group, was working without being paid; he was doing for his King what others would do only for cash. To a degree, espionage sickens and corrupts Ashenden, however aloof he seems to remain from the action and however immune to rough consequences. Maugham was to say that he had met a great many statesmen and politicians and that he had never found them to be particularly intelligent; to judge from those who carried out their orders, they were more likely to be possessed of a bland ruthlessness and a cultivated lack of humane scruple. Maugham's failure to adhere to any literary school, either in the 'artistic' twenties or in the 'political' thirties, may be attributed to his diet of lotus, to his having been spoiled by money and self-indulgence, but it should also be noted that he had large experience of the world at the dirty end of the stick and that his medical background, no less than his complacent modesty, made him as dubious of panaceas as of ideologies. He was in the habit of saying, with more frequency than originality, that men were not all of one piece. When writers insist on a platitude, it is usually because it is one that the clever ignore and also because it is one that applies to them.

Secret Agent (1936), with Madeleine Carroll, was a film made by Alfred Hitchcock from the Ashenden stories.

Hugh Walpole (on the stool) in a London art gallery.

If the retreat to the Villa Mauresque distanced Maugham from the world of English letters, it did not deprive him of a shrewd notion of what went on within its parish. In 1930 he published *Cakes and Ale*. The opening of the book has a jaunty, colloquial tone: 'When someone calls you on the telephone and leaves a message that you should call him back, and that it is very important, it is usually more important for him than it is for you. . . .' It is also the tone of a narrator who need no longer introduce or justify himself. Willie Ashenden, for it is again he, is presented as a somewhat sarcastic and frigid figure, but Maugham's *alter ego* here is by no means the mere victim who was Philip Carey or the minor celebrity he was in *The Moon and Sixpence*; he has become an established man of letters. His affectations of insignificance serve merely to underline the ridiculous self-importance of Alroy Kear, the literary climber whose telephone call begins the book. Kear has been approached to write a biography of Edward Driffield, the recently dead Grand Old Man of

English literature. Driffield was surely a portrait of Thomas Hardy, 'the good little Thomas Hardy' in the terms of Henry James's faint praise, and Kear was even more unmistakably based on Hugh Walpole, the darling of the lending libraries and the one-time *protégé* of that same Henry James who had not seen fit to include the young Somerset Maugham in his roster of Younger Novelists back in 1913. Revenge is sweet and its sweetness was not of the kind Maugham's teeth were able to resist. Indeed, the greater part of his *œuvre* could be read as an exercise in revenge; even his agnosticism seemed often to reproach God for not being there to listen to his reasonable grievances. ('I'm glad I don't believe in God. When I look at the misery of the world and its bitterness I think no belief can be more ignoble.' Now what have You got to say for Yourself?)

Hugh Walpole was shattered by the portrait Maugham painted of him. Here was a gross flatterer of reviewers, a tailored *arriviste* with ludicrously snobbish tastes, a toady both humourless and opportunistic, a writer of no serious purpose interested only in the library public and the social scene. If Walpole had been sensible, he would have laughed gaily and then kept quiet. But if he was many of the things that Maugham said (wasn't Maugham?), he was also sensitive. He squawked. And the squawk of a celebrity was music to the gossips and to the book-buying public. *Cakes and Ale* was a hit. Maugham later proclaimed disingenuously that the characters in *Cakes and Ale* were really all based on aspects of himself. What writer would not claim the same? One begins with others, one ends with oneself. Certainly Maugham was not above entertaining reviewers. Michael Ayrton recalled going with his father, Gerald Gould, the *Observer* fiction critic, to lunch with Maugham at Claridges. The twelve-year-old Ayrton was baffled by the French menu and asked for the only dish written in English: smoked salmon. The successful man of letters looked balefully at the boy. 'Much too expensive,' he said.

There are few novelists who can claim never to have attempted to subvert the course of critical justice, though Walpole certainly carried this subversion to unprecedentedly diplomatic lengths. If it was deplorable that Maugham should pick him out, it was also irresistible. The picture of Thomas Hardy, who had died in 1929, was more respectful; Driffield was a genius, at least, but here too there was scandalous stuff, for he was depicted as the victim of a second wife who tidied up his private life and ran his affairs in so prim and proper a way that she bled all the life out of him and left him with only the consolations of longevity, that prerequisite of literary eminence in England. But if there was a scandalous (and delicious) insolence in Maugham's disdain for the proprieties, there was also a character who captured the public's imagination, Rosie, the amoral barmaid who was Driffield's first wife, unfaithful, amorous Rosie, the fountain of life for all the men who came in contact with her and who, in one of the most memorable of all love scenes, a scene which combines candour with reticence, gives herself to Willie out of pity and affection, out of the goodness of her heart.

In a novel so shamelessly *à clef* (Maugham denied at the time that Walpole was in his mind, but later acknowledged that he lied) it is natural to look for some original for Rosie. Nor did Maugham deny that there was one, though he did not openly admit it until 1950, in his introduction to the Modern Library Edition (where he also insisted, unconvincingly, that Driffield was not based on Hardy); he said that Rosie

Thomas Hardy; a portrait by Augustus John.

Peter Paul Rubens, *Hélène Fourment in a Fur Robe*.

had been an actress and unhappily married. He met her, many years before, in the days when he went to the house of Mrs G. W. Steevens. In his Notebook for 1904, there are the following entries:

She had something of the florid colouring of Helena Fourment, the second wife of Rubens, that blonde radiancy, with eyes blue as the sea at mid-summer and hair like corn under the August sun, but a greater delicacy withal. And she hadn't Helena's unhappy leaning to obesity.

She was a woman of ripe and abundant charms, *rosy* of cheek and fair of hair, with eyes blue as the summer sea, with rounded lines and full breasts. She leaned somewhat to the overblown. She belonged to that type of woman that Rubens has set down forever in the ravishing person of Helena Fourment.

The elaborate mixture of the platitudinous and the high-flown suggests sincere, almost embarrassed, admiration. For a full account of who Rosie might have been, the reader is recommended to Robert Calder's Appendix A, where all the details are lucidly marshalled. Maugham varied his account of Rosie (he was unreliable about the date of her death), but there seems small doubt that the woman he loved was Ethelwyn Sylvia Jones, the daughter of the playwright, Henry Arthur Jones; she had been a frequent visitor at Merton Abbey, Mrs Steevens's house. She had appeared on the stage, with some success, and took the part of the maid in Maugham's *Penelope* in 1909, for which performance she was praised in *The Sunday Times* by J. C. Grein. The clinching evidence comes from Sir Gerald Kelly who painted 'Sue' Jones's portrait several times; one such is described, with the most minor discrepancies only, in *Cakes and Ale*. Sir Gerald confirmed to Mr Calder that Willie had always admired this particular picture. In a conversation with Garson Kanin, Maugham confessed that he had only once in his life proposed marriage to a woman, and that the woman was not the one he married. It was Ethelwyn, and the proposal was almost certainly made in Chicago in 1913. Maugham was in the United States for one of his productions, and Miss Jones (who had divorced Montague Leaveaux a few years earlier) was pursuing her own acting career in America. She and Maugham had been lovers since 1905, though there is no evidence that the affair was based on a singular attachment. Certainly if Rosie was an affectionate mistress, she was not an exclusive one. Maugham claimed that she would have married him, had it not been that she was at the time pregnant by another man. On 13 December 1913, Ethelwyn married Angus McDonnell, the second son of the sixth Earl of Antrim, who was in America on business. 'Rosie' died in 1948, and her husband, after being awarded the C.B. and C.M.G. in the First World War, became a Conservative M.P. (for Dartford) and was an Honorary Attaché at the British Embassy in Washington during the Second World War. He died in 1966 at the age of eighty-four. Maugham's reluctance to name the object of his love argues a nice sense of propriety rather than any coyness. Hugh Walpole, in an understandable outburst, claimed that Rosie was the only fictional character in *Cakes and Ale* and maintained, according to Beverley Nichols, that 'there'd never been a Rosie in [Maugham's] life and never would be'. It is to Maugham's credit, surely, that he never disclosed the evidence of a heterosexual passion which might, in the cockeyed morality of our time, have reflected well on him, though at the expense of his beloved's good name.

Ethelwyn Sylvia Jones; a portrait by
Gerald Kelly.

There are two minor curiosities in the matter of Rose. One is that he gave that
name to the girl whom his hero loves in 'The Artistic Temperament of Stephen
Carey', written before he met 'Sue', and the other is that there is, in *Of Human
Bondage*, a boy called Rose, a schoolfellow at Tercanbury, for whom the hero
experiences what is plainly very close to a homosexual love and who rejects him,
without any particular malice, in favour of another. The notion that Mildred is a
more sombre (or more realistic) portrayal of Rosie, after the disappointment of
Chicago, will not do. In any case, Maugham was never embittered by 'Sue's'
rejection of him, which he may have regarded as the result of one of fate's ironic twists,
rather than a personal refusal; he continued to speak of her as the one woman whom
he had loved and who had, we need not doubt, merited that love. Noël Coward in
his late play, *A Song at Twilight*, seems to echo Hugh Walpole's charge that
Maugham's heterosexual passions, to which he refers in his autobiographical
writings, were fantasies or feints, but Coward may have been alluding to his own life
(as writers will), as much as to Willie's. Did he not claim that Gertie Lawrence had
only ever been in love with him and never with her husband?

Cakes and Ale was enthusiastically reviewed. Mark Van Doren admired it;
Alexander Woollcott called it a masterpiece; and, in England, V. S. Pritchett and
Cyril Connolly, bright young men both, were hardly less enthusiastic. It is still
highly readable. The intercutting between the adolescent memories of Willie
Ashenden and the intrigues of literary London displays a mastery of narrative skill
that puts the seal on its author's reputation for elegant economy. The story was
televised as recently as 1974 and the characters remained both fresh and convincing.
No wonder it was said that Alroy Kear ruined the last ten years of Walpole's life! Yet
the book does not often rate more than a passing mention in studies of the English
novel. It was, however, not merely the scandal (which provoked a parody called *Gin
and Bitters* by Elinor Mordaunt under the pseudonym 'A. Riposte') and the candid
sentimentality which account for its success. Maugham was not to include Proust in
his list of the best ten novelists, probably because he was too philosophical for the
average reader, but he was a profound admirer of *A la Recherche du Temps Perdu* and
in *Cakes and Ale* there is an Arcadian element: Blackstable echoes Combray. A
sensitive adolescent (and how well Maugham catches the priggishness, no less than
the *gaucherie*, of his young self!) enters a world more complicated and more painful
than he knows and grows up to realize the vanity of life and the fugitive nature of both
fame and beauty. Irony here serves to flavour, not to corrode, the past. *Cakes and Ale*
has an elegiac tone that deserves recognition. If Maugham was still not rated as
important, it was partly because he continued to be prolific. E. M. Forster ceased
writing novels in 1926 and lived until 1970; with every year of silence, his reputation
grew. Was his homosexuality part of the reason for his retirement? The cynicism and
the coldness which critics found in Maugham were, perhaps, devices for avoiding too
much self-revelation; by assuming a moral neutrality he was able to maintain his
fecundity. Forster's more committed manner may have led to a crisis which
Maugham was able to bypass. Maugham's medical mode did not require of him that
he be himself healthy; so long as the doctor can diagnose with clarity and keep his
personal peculiarities out of the consulting-room, he can continue to practise.

The flow of work continued with both plays and short stories. *The Bread Winner*
was written and produced in 1930, with Jack Hawkins, Marie Löhr and the young
Peggy Ashcroft. The theme was once again that of a man who breaks away from his
conventional and leeching family and refuses to go on keeping them. The most
spiritual of Maugham's heroes – Charles Strickland, who cares only for Art, and
Larry Darrell, who finds Faith – rise above money, but he found it at the bottom of
most people's motives. One may, of course, find a psychological explanation of this
peculiar to Maugham, but no very different notion underlies Balzac's view of the
world, and what may plausibly be attributed to anal fixation could as well be put
down to a French literary diet.

Another kind of break for freedom was to be found in the volume of *Six Stories
Written in the First Person Singular*, which was published in 1931 (with the usual
10,000 volumes in the first run on both sides of the Atlantic). One of the stories, 'The
Alien Corn', concerns an Anglicized Jewish family whose golden boy, a son who
looks as Anglo-Saxon as his parents would wish they were, decides to quit the ranks
of the moneyed and become a concert pianist. Maugham has some ironic fun at the
expense of his oh-so-British Jews, but there is little evidence of the anti-Semitism of

A scene from *Alien Corn*, one of the four short stories which made up the successful film, *Quartet*, 1948.

which he was sometimes accused. (Jews often figure amiably in his work, and in his life; Ferdy Rabenstein, in the same story, is a highly attractive, if flamboyant, figure and a man can scarcely like New York literary society and have no use for Jews.) The irony of the story is that the would-be pianist's brother, who looks like a caricature of a Jew, wants nothing more than to be the Anglicized gentleman which the pianist disdains to be. The pianist turns out to be no genius and commits suicide. The twist is melodramatic and the family can scarcely be said to be typical, whatever that is, yet there is a measure of sympathy in the portrayal of these Jewish *parvenus* which is not to be found in more 'important' writers of the period.

Maugham could assume, with great ease, the condescending prejudices of his time, but he had no truck with the brutal discrimination of those who advocated, however slyly, the extinction (or therapeutic expropriation) of those who were different. Here his homosexuality was perhaps, as with Byron, the humanizing factor; Maugham, if methodically derisive, did not indulge in the self-made mandarin malice of Eliot and Pound, the murderous partiality of Wyndham Lewis and Belloc, the dotty theorizing of D. H. Lawrence or the cocky fantasies of H. G. Wells. All of these believed, in some degree, in purging society, not only of Jews, but of troublesome, dissident people of one kind and another. More popular novelists and thriller-writers shared their infantile notions in a coarser and more vicious way. It was left to Kipling to realize that Gunga Din was at times the better man, and to Maugham to recognize the multiplicity of life; both deprecated the arrogance of the British as they strutted their narrow stage. If some emphasis is placed here on Maugham's homosexuality, it should be remembered that, to a degree, it was a liberation, no less than a source of shame. Philip Toynbee remarks that when he was a Communist he tried dutifully, and vainly, to make contact with members of the working class, while a homosexual friend, although on the right wing in politics, managed effortlessly to achieve the *rapport* which the ideologically correct Toynbee found impossible. The freemasonry which the self-righteous find so deplorable, in Jews or homosexuals, can be a powerful source of both generosity and insight.

Another substantial *conte*, 'The Book Bag', appeared in 1932, and formed part of the collection entitled *Ah King* (1933). Most of the stories published in volume form had, of course, been printed elsewhere first. American magazines, like *Cosmopolitan*, as Scott Fitzgerald had found out, paid very well indeed for the right material. Maugham's experience in the theatre made it easy for him to sugar the astringent medicine he offered the public. He was not so softened as Fitzgerald was by the easy pickings, but he continued to pick them. 'The Book Bag' was actually rejected as uncommercial by *Cosmopolitan*, where Maugham published many stories over the years, but when Ray Long, the editor, came to publish a volume of his best twenty, he realized that 'The Book Bag' merited a place. Long asked Maugham's permission to include it in the anthology and, grateful for many kindnesses, Maugham agreed. The story was already due to be published, by Orioli in Florence, in a limited edition, but there was unlikely to be any conflict. Raymond Toole Stott, whose exemplary bibliography is a mine of Maughamiana under its strict orthodoxy, remarks that Maugham was in some sense responsible for Ray Long's death. The editor read the typescript of *The Moon and Sixpence* and was moved to throw up his job and go to the South Seas and paint. He did so for a number of years and then came to the conclusion that he had no talent, whereupon he killed himself.

The Narrow Corner was Maugham's main published work in 1932. His fame was such that the book was serialized on both sides of the Atlantic and once again sold very well. But it has a weary air of professional competence, rehearsing its well-made plot without any of the nice ironies and passionate involvement of *Cakes and Ale*. There is no feeling that it was a book that cried out to be written; it has the taste of ashes. Laurence Brander, whose guide to Maugham's works deserves recognition, thinks otherwise. There are, of course, meanings to be teased from it. Doctor Saunders, another of Maugham's wryly detached medical men, an opium addict and a very discreet homosexual, is the narrator; his sense of the fleetingness of things (the entire first chapter consists of the sentence: 'All this happened a long time ago') informs the book with a framework of allegorical sententiousness; his moral nihilism is redeemed by his respect for goodness. Goodness was the *summum bonum* to which Maugham's philosophical bent – he read metaphysics all his life – inclined him to defer above all things. There seems to be a measure of guarded *naïveté* in his belief that it was a natural phenomenon, like some rare Alpine flower, in front of which one could but gasp. The origin of this notion of goodness is to be found, one suspects, in an inversion of *fin-de-siècle* decadence no less than in the philosophy of G. E. Moore who held, in *Principia Ethica*, that there was some mysterious connection between goodness and beauty, especially male beauty.

Captain Nichols, the scoundrelly, cheerful captain of the boat which carries the amiable young murderer Fred around the South Seas while he waits for the fuss to die down in Australia, where he has killed his mistress's husband, also appears, briefly, in *The Moon and Sixpence*. Did the shadow of Balzac lead Maugham to dream of a Human Comedy of his own, in which each volume played off against another? He certainly shared Balzac's belief that what mattered was to build up an *œuvre*, not to produce a few blinding flashes in the pan. To this end, *The Narrow Corner* indeed serves; the South Seas, with their measureless distances, their human wreckage rendered insignificant against the magnificence of the islands and the indifference of nature, are charted, once again, with a masterly certainty. Maugham's pessimism here reaches its nadir. For if Saunders and Nichols, both burnt-out cases in their ways, manage to survive the long voyage, it is because they are without illusions or hopes. Passion leads only to disaster and death, as is emphasized by the bodies that litter their Odyssey.

The Narrow Corner may also testify to a turning-point in Maugham's own life. Certainly, so far as his literary life is concerned, a crisis was approaching. In 1933 he retired from the theatre. His last two plays are deeply sombre in their different ways. *For Services Rendered*, put on in London at the Globe Theatre on 1 November 1932, had Flora Robson, Ralph Richardson and Cedric Hardwicke in the cast. It was a savage and brilliant attack on the illusions of the post-war world; it exposed once again the futility of heroism and the self-deception of those who uttered pious sentiments while others fought their battles. Once again there is a wounded hero and once again he embarrasses his middle-class family by his bitter despair. Maugham had long ago seen that suffering did not ennoble, as the comfortable incumbents of the Church of England liked to declare, and that it was more likely to shrivel than to expand the soul. He rammed the lesson home with all his malign force and he cannot have expected that the public would like it. They did not; no more did they appreciate the lesson of his last play, *Sheppey*, despite the amusing first act in which Sheppey, the Cockney barber, is shown practising his trade in a smart West End salon. When he wins the Irish Sweep, his family promptly assume that they are on easy street, but an encounter with a prostitute makes him realize how wretched is the life of London's derelicts. He decides to give the money away. His family's jubilation changes to fury; they plan to have him certified. (The 1936 film, *Mr Deeds Goes to Town*, used much the same idea.) Once again society's revenge against anyone who does not share its mousey values becomes the theme of Maugham's drama. He has travelled a long way from *A Man of Honour*, but it has been a round trip.

His last plays were not hits, but the decision to renounce the theatre, which he declared prevented him from writing the things he wanted, can scarcely have been imposed upon him only by the narrow tastes of the managers or the public. He had had enough. The form which constricted him, that of the well-made play built to West End specifications, was one that he had chosen for himself and from which he showed no large signs of wishing to stray. It is true that the Lord Chamberlain still exercised authority over what might and might not be said, but nothing in the style or content of Maugham's prose after 1933 suggests that the rupture was caused by a desire to say forbidden things in new or outrageous ways. Perhaps it was simply that he wished now to please himself, rather than others.

After *Ah King*, the collection which included 'The Book Bag' and 'The Back of Beyond', came work on *Don Fernando*, about his first love, Spain. There are indeed signs here of a modest change of tone. The style is still precise and elegant, but a certain sly discursiveness is present. Indeed the whole book is a discursion, for its subject is a book about Spain which the author finally decided he was not competent to write. Thus, although it strikes no innovatory postures, it has something in common with Nabokov's *The Real Life of Sebastian Knight*, which also manages to hold the attention rapt while never actually reaching its supposed subject. The search for goodness, or salvation, is implicit in the book's admirable, if sometimes excessively contrived, style. *Don Fernando* is reflective writing which does not fail to be either readable or informative; if Maugham's appetite for what Jeremy Taylor (whose style he imitated in his first book about Spain) called 'Holy Living' seems to sort ill with the lavish style in which he lived, the contradiction was not keenly felt by the author. He comforted himself that artists had always liked luxury and there is in *Don Fernando* an account of El Greco which seeks to reconcile the self-indulgence and the genius at home in him. There is also a slightly condescending disquisition on the homosexual, with his taste for the gaudy. (One recalls that Maugham's brother, invited to admire a splendid ormolu table in Maugham's drawing-room, remarked scathingly, 'A bit florid, isn't it?') Despite its charm and its air of learning worn with agreeable lightness, *Don Fernando* gained Maugham no admiration in the highest academic quarters. A Cambridge critic, E.M. Wilson, was sarcastic in *Scrutiny*:

Briefly speaking, Mr Maugham has no qualifications as a literary critic except honesty and a flair for the striking in narrative. . . . There is a blindness to artistic excellence which invalidates almost all his judgements. I think that he misrepresents most of the authors that he quotes and he quotes widely. His facts are not always reliable and the authorities are a heterogeneous bunch.

Hard indeed is the way of the popularizer in the eyes of the stringent. However, the heterogeneity of which Mr Wilson complained was elegantly moulded together by Maugham's sceptical sentimentality. He may have misunderstood Spain but his affection for it was enduring and it may be said that honesty is not always a common quality in critics.

You will look in vain in Maugham's Spain for any attitude or even reference to the social upheavals of the time. The love, and it was deep, that Maugham felt for Spain was for the Spain of the great religious mystics, above all Loyola and St Teresa and for the great writers, for the picaresque and the picturesque. He steered clear of politics as he did of judgments (here again the model was Balzac, whose work was none the less, like Maugham's, instinct with opinions) and if he regretted the victory of that Christian gentleman General Franco, he never said so. His visits to Spain continued.

His work affected to a certain timelessness. He belonged now to literature, not to life. He had, he once said, often enjoyed writing; he had never enjoyed living. Such remarks seem ungrateful in one who consumed so many sweet grapes, but Maugham's life can never be understood if he is taken to have aimed only at riches and, by calculation, to have got what he wanted. François Mauriac once said that no

Opposite, Maugham's Spain; the convent of St Teresa of Avila in Seville.

Maugham with friends in Austria;
Gerald Haxton is second from the right.

large success is ever unwarranted. This notion, which a cynic might take as a covert plug for the Catholic Church (a similar creed can be read into certain of Graham Greene's attitudes), cannot be accepted too unhesitatingly, but those who jeer at Maugham's limitations are, in fairness, bound to ask themselves how so flawed a writer commanded so wide and so faithful a public. The truth is that people trusted him. He did not inspire them (unless they were unlucky, like Ray Long) but he could comfort no less than entertain them. He was a popularizer – *Don Fernando* is a masterpiece at least of palatability – and if such men are seldom well regarded by those who carry their learning ponderously, it required a sustained effort of reading and refinement, as well as all the travelling and the questioning, to manage so balanced and so authoritative a manner. Alec Waugh wrote of him as a kind of father-figure, understanding and uncensorious, a consultant psychiatrist perhaps, about whose own life it would be impertinent to inquire but on whom one could rely for the most intimate, as well as the most commonsensical, advice. The constant success of his stories (*Cosmopolitans* was published in 1936) owed much to his original admiration for Maupassant – 'A String of Beads' could scarcely come closer to what is traditionally regarded as the sincerest form of flattery – but it owed no less to the consistent persona of the author, whose vintage wisdom was uncorked, if only by the half-bottle, for all who would pay his modest price.

There was now, and henceforth would always be, an air of retirement about him; he went early into a sort of protracted, prophylactic senescence. Even in the middle, a wise novelist starts tidying up the ends. However, his energies were far from spent; even as an Old Party he had stamina. In 1936, on the suggestion of Rudyard Kipling, he went to the West Indies where, as in so many parts of the world, the Union

Jack still flew and the White Man bore his burden. Although society in the Caribbean colonies must have had much in common with that of Malaya, he did not find anything there which he cared to turn into fiction. There was nothing of the remoteness of the South Seas and none of the industrious despair of the planters in Malaya. He went on to Guiana and his determined curiosity took him also to Devil's Island, where the French still maintained the penal colony to which Dreyfus had once been sent. The Governor housed him in a little cottage with two murderers to look after him. He watched the executioner rehearsing his gruesome duties by putting under the knife of the guillotine a banana stalk of the same thickness as a man's neck. He was amused to discover that, behind all the passions and the violence of the convicts and especially of the murderers, there nearly always lay a banal financial motive. Devil's Island provided him with more stories than anywhere else on that trip.

In 1937 came *Theatre*, a celebration of a bitch-goddess by one who had worshipped at the shrine of many such a leading lady and had been well compensated for his devotion. Julia (Noël Coward gave the same name to the actress heroine of *Hay Fever*) is a type rather than an individual, but there are indeed many actresses of her kind, comfortable in playing a part, fickle and capricious in life. The novel is facile and amusing; it was itself made into a play by Guy Bolton after the war and was expertly played by Jessie Royce Landis. No one would guess that the book was written in a deepening world crisis. Yet if Maugham lived in lotus land, he lived also in France and knew it well. He was later to diagnose the reasons for France's collapse with considerable acumen. He must have guessed what was coming. Meanwhile, in 1938 he went to India. Perhaps he had always regarded it as Kipling's manor, for this was his first visit. He saw a different world from that described by the poet of Empire, whose work he so admired and for whose collected stories, at the nadir of their fame, he wrote a properly laudatory introduction. Maugham did not write about India in the same fashion that he did about the British in Malaya and the South Seas; he reserved this new landscape for *The Razor's Edge*. It was less the social charades of the Raj that intrigued him than the extraordinary spiritual distinction of Indian philosophers and ascetics. 'As soon as the Maharajahs realized that I didn't want to go on tiger hunts but that I was interested in seeing poets and philosophers, they were very helpful,' he told Alec Waugh. He planned to return to India in the autumn of 1939, but by that time France was at war. What most impressed him in the Indian sages was their liberation from sensuality. The need for such gratification bound Maugham always to others. He did not deny himself, but he recognized that the detachment for which he longed was, like true wisdom, impossible so long as a man remained the slave of his desires. He once recommended a morality which accepted how most men behaved and called that good, but he had come to see that goodness was not, after all, a common quality. He now took the view that it depended on a kind of fineness which was beyond the carnal. To this extent, those who see in him a religious streak are not wrong. He was attracted too by the doctrine of transmigration of souls, the notion that they pass from one living thing to another and progress to the highest rewards of bliss only through a process of merited refinement. What could be fairer than such a system of spiritual promotion? Everything was to be said for believing it, save that it was unbelievable.

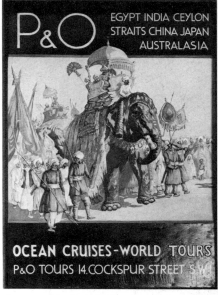

A poster of the P. & O. lines (1930), which provided not only Maugham's various passages to India and the Far East, but also the setting for several of his stories.

Frederick Herbert Maugham, Lord Chancellor, Somerset Maugham's brother; a portrait by Gerald Kelly.

His general reflections on the soul and on life were presented to the public in *The Summing Up*, which was published in 1938. Although the judicial title was amply warranted by the matter, a further sly reason for it may have crossed Maugham's mind. In the same year, Frederick Herbert Maugham was created first Viscount and became Lord Chancellor of England, the highest law officer in the land. It can hardly have delighted him to see his writer brother appropriate the legal function of summing up. In the book, Mr Maugham claimed to be concluding his *œuvre*. He enjoyed the opportunity of donning the wig and robe and telling the world a thing or two. One might have been forgiven for imagining that some irreversible disease had given him only a few months to live; the tone is brave as well as dry. He was in fact sixty-four years old and he had another twenty-seven years to live.

Once again it is as though he were rehearsing a departure both desired and feared. How splendid it would be to leave life on such a gracious note, like a man thanking a hostess for a party which he has not wholly enjoyed but where he has met some interesting people! *The Summing Up* is largely autobiography, but of a reflective, dispassionate kind. The mature man appears as detached as the aged Sophocles who, free of the desire for women, felt that he had escaped from the clutches of a wild beast. He muses over success and failure and illustrates them with pithy incident. He is lofty but not high-faluting. He gives sensible advice, especially on the craft of writing. Dryden and Hazlitt are his two models of English prose; Swift's rhythms are admirable but a little predictable and he cleaves to the view that good prose should be like the conversation of civilized men. He is not boastful, but one senses a certain satisfaction in having made one's own way in the world and in having ended somewhere near the top. He is conscious of not having pleased all the critics all the time, but money – that sixth sense without which you cannot enjoy the other five – has its compensations. The book was admired not only by the public, but also by so unsparing a critic as Virginia Woolf who sent her congratulations through the egregious Harold Nicolson, a guest at the Villa Mauresque soon after publication. It could be said that Maugham's claims to be but an amateur philosopher were justified by his unremarkable observations on metaphysics, yet one retains a certain sympathy with his suspicion that the metaphysician resembles a man who climbs a mountain only to find the view from the top swathed in cloud. One cannot blame him for announcing, on coming down again, that he has had a spectacular revelation. *The Summing Up* has something of the earthy condescension that might be found in a shrewd judge who, as Maugham inelegantly but humanely recommended, kept a roll of lavatory paper on the bench beside him, an inanimate surrogate for the Roman slave who whispered to triumphant generals, 'Remember you too are a man.' His final word comes, as one might expect, from a Spaniard, Fray Luis de León: 'The beauty of life, he says, is nothing but this, that each should act in conformity with his nature and his business.'

There is a sort of lordly modesty here which makes no large claims and yet indicates that the author may deserve a place alongside those genial humanists like Montaigne, who lived in his tower and yet never pretended that it was made of ivory, and Hazlitt, whose distinction of style did not preclude an appreciation of others and who never allowed a taste for excellence to desiccate his palate. In *The Summing Up* Maugham laid claim to a place among the wise and he was wise enough to do so

Harold Nicolson and his wife, Vita Sackville-West.

without posturing and without stridency. It might indeed have been a fitting epitaph for a long career, but the career was not yet dead.

He must have begun *Christmas Holiday* almost before the ink was dry on *The Summing Up*. It was in a sense a new beginning, for it took account, at this late date, of the political situation in the world at large. It has a young hero, Charlie Mason, son of amiable middle-class parents, who is given a ticket to go and enjoy himself in Paris, and discovers the snake-pit of a Europe pullulating with the violence and venom of totalitarianism. The narrative is an uneven amalgam of satire on English complacency and horrified fascination with the dark passions that threaten it. The smooth detachment of *The Summing Up* yields to a rejuvenating, if uneven, urgency. The attempt to make the message of doom into something the libraries will find acceptable tends to give the last trump the tones of a Geraldo band, but the purpose remains an honourable one. Maugham recognized a ruthlessness far beyond the capacity of the insular British to understand; the lotus had not, after all, rendered him lazy or blind. He might have done better, from the literary point of view, not to publish *Christmas Holiday*, but the warning was as timely as it was futile. In the last months before the outbreak of war, he kept a phial of sleeping pills close at hand. He did not intend to be captured alive by the Germans. Having reacted with honourable vigour when Lion Feuchtwanger, expelled and deprived of his German nationality by the Nazis, was detained by the French authorities, Maugham was on the Gestapo's black list. He was too modest to claim that he personally had secured Feuchtwanger's release, but it followed promptly on his intercession with Jean Giraudoux, the playwright who was also Minister of Information. On the other hand, thousands of Spanish refugees were in concentration camps in south-western

France. What appeals did he launch on their behalf? Maugham's solicitude tended to be for individuals and most of the individuals he knew were celebrated ones.

As the crisis deepened, the French began, belatedly, to take steps to protect their coasts. A deputation came from Toulon to ask whether Monsieur Maugham would allow naval guns to be sited on his land. He paid tribute to the long hospitality that France had given him and acceded readily. When he was asked how much money he wanted for the inconvenience, he said that he could not possibly accept anything since the safety of France itself was involved. The deputation regarded this unGallic generosity with the deepest suspicion. The guns never came to the Villa Mauresque. But war did. For all his apprehensions of doom, until the last moment Maugham curtailed neither the style nor the scale of his entertaining. Like the Gerald Murphys years before, he took the view that living well was the best revenge. In the summer of 1939 the Windsors were guests at the Villa Mauresque. Gerald Haxton continued to mix his excellent cocktails and to behave outrageously. There was swimming and bridge and tennis. The world that had suffered a stroke in 1914 was about to be stricken even more severely, but the aristocracy of wealth and talent and beauty took its last summer holidays with the usual insouciance. Epicurus did not leave his garden until he had to. Once the war had begun, things went, of course, as badly as Maugham had feared they would. The French were *pourris*: 'If a nation values anything more than its freedom, it will lose its freedom; and the irony is that if it is comfort or money that it values more, it will lose that too.'

If Maugham foresaw France's ruin, he did not vaunt himself on the accuracy of his hunch. After a premature departure from Cap Ferrat, in Haxton's boat, the *Sara*, they put in at Cassis and then at Bandol. Maugham wearied of flight, took a taxi back to the Villa Mauresque and proceeded from there to Paris where he collected material for a series of articles which were later issued in a paperback under the title *France at War*; he did his best, *malgré tout*, to put the French in a flattering light. He was in England for three months during the early part of 1940 and returned to the Riviera just in time for the German invasion of Belgium and Holland and for the ordering of 20,000 tulip bulbs for autumn setting at the Villa Mauresque. One is reminded of Leonard Woolf, planting irises in his garden when Virginia told him that Hitler was fulminating on the wireless. He decided not to go in and listen; the irises would be there when Hitler was dead and buried. Maugham seemed to have had something of the same horticultural faith.

However, Hitler was still very much alive. Goebbels found time to denounce Maugham personally, adducing Ashenden as evidence of the perfidy of the British. Maugham did not stay to face his club-footed accuser. He headed for Nice where he was lucky enough to find a ship about to sail for England. She was a 4,000-ton collier, filthy and packed with refugees. Maugham had little money and no choice. After the war he was to startle Garson Kanin by a casual disclosure that he always carried an attaché-case with $100,000 in it. Wasn't it very risky? Very, but he had been caught short once, and once was enough.

The journey was dirty, dull and dangerous. But Maugham was nothing if not a practical traveller. True, it was a long time since he had not travelled in some state, but he was no stranger to roughing it; he had always taken the best accommodation available on his journeys, but what sounded luxurious in the days before jet-travel

Garson Kanin and Ruth Gordon, who became close friends of Maugham during the war years that he spent in the United States.

A French family fleeing from the German advance in 1940.

would hardly satisfy a modern package-tourist and what was merely tolerable would now seem positively primitive. He made the best of a bad job and passed the long, crowded days in telling his fellow refugees stories. They sat round him on the deck. Had he not always said that fiction was as old as man and that it was the story-teller's art to entertain, not to educate his audience? One wonders if he ever stammered during that strange, voluntary scheherazade. Did he, like many with the same affliction, find that his tongue was untied when he impersonated his characters and told of their adventures, even when one of the characters was that cool customer Mr Maugham and the adventures his own?

The apocalypse which he had foreseen in *Christmas Holiday* had come about. He was temporarily homeless, though he scarcely lacked a roof for his head, and he may well have thought that he would never again see the Villa Mauresque. The writer has one sovereign cure for such anxieties; he can work. In 1940 Maugham published another collection of stories, all of them extremely slight and distinctly amusing. *The Times* had reviewed his last collection under the medical rubric 'The Mixture as Before'. What title could be more appropriate for the new one? In the Foreword he said, 'I have now written between eighty and ninety short stories, I shall not write any more.' When he published *Creatures of Circumstance* in 1947, he claimed that 'any' was a misprint for 'many'. He liked to be thought of as a man of his word.

While he was in London, Beldy, the widow of his brother Charles, visited him at the Dorchester Hotel. She had been the model for the saintly mother in *The Sacred Flame*, but her last sight of him was to be disagreeable. She lamented the fall of France, where she had lived most of her married life, and Willie flew into a passion.

Maugham photographed at his desk in the Dorchester Hotel, London, before his departure for the United States in 1940.

Had he been bottling up his own regrets and so found her lamentation too close to his heart? He and Beldy never saw each other again. Emotion always seems to have upset him ('What the hell do I care?' was his likely response to declarations of deep feeling) and it requires no great intuition to guess that it was fear of his own tears which led him so to reprobate those of others.

He left London for New York in October 1940. He had had some experience of the Blitz – he dined with the Duff Coopers in Westminster during a particularly severe air raid and they sat imperturbably listening to a Haydn Trio – but it was probably less fear of discomfort than the lack of Gerald Haxton's company that drove him to take the Clipper to America. Haxton had stayed behind on the Riviera, packing up valuables at the Villa Mauresque and coolly making arrangements which were to stand his employer in good stead after the war. When Haxton had finished, he made his way to Lisbon and flew to New York. Not even as a refugee could he be sure of a welcome in the London he always insisted he hated but from which, Robin Maugham points out, he always ordered his Bond Street cigarettes, his Savile Row suits and his Jermyn Street shirts.

At La Guardia Airport Maugham was met by his publisher, Nelson Doubleday and his wife. As soon as he had passed through immigration, he asked for a bourbon old-fashioned. In Garson Kanin's words, 'He drank [it] with great relish and thanked the Doubledays. Whereupon he took an ampoule of poison out of his vest [waistcoat] pocket, put it on the floor, and crushed it under his heel, saying, "I won't need this now, Nelson."'

In 1941 Doubleday (and Heinemann) published what is almost certainly his worst novel, *Up at the Villa*, a pot-boiler that never even simmers. He claimed to have been seduced into writing it by a commission from a magazine which then rejected it on censorious grounds. There followed *The Hour before the Dawn*, also a commission, intended to demonstrate the spirit of the British in wartime adversity. It depicted the comfortable fortunes of a family of the upper middle class, living in a country-house. He must have thought it even worse than *Up at the Villa* for he never allowed it to be published in England. In writing of Britain under fire, he was trying, of course, to do his bit, but he chose a strange bit to do. Despite (or because of) its weaknesses, the book was filmed, in 1944, with Veronica Lake and Franchot Tone.

At first, he stayed at the Ritz Hotel in New York, on a stipend of $1,500 a month; it was hardly slumming it, but he deliberately refused to take more, feeling that ostentation ill became a man whose country was fighting for its life. He went with Gerald Haxton to Hollywood, which he described as 'like having nothing to eat but candy'. It was while he was in California that his wit earned him the enmity of Garson Kanin's friend, Spencer Tracy. Tracy was filming *Dr Jekyll and Mr Hyde*, and for the part of Mr Hyde he elected to rely less on horrific make-up than on his acting to give the impression of evil. Maugham was taken to the set and watched a scene being shot. George Cukor explained to him how Tracy was approaching the double part of Jekyll and Hyde. During a take, in which Tracy was giving a chilling impression of evil, Maugham said, 'Which one is he now?'

Maugham was himself very sensitive to rudeness and in society had impeccable, even courtly, manners, but the memory of Oscar and the epigrammatists of the nineties was always with him; he could no more resist being witty (not at all the same thing as being rude) than could one of his fat ladies of Antibes resist a cream-puff. He soon left the house he had rented in Beverly Hills, where there was 'no one to talk to' and, in December, he went to Parker's Ferry, a modest guest-house built especially for him on the Doubledays' plantation in South Carolina. Gerald Haxton soon grew bored with the quiet life and took a job doing war work in Washington. Maugham was alone most of the time. He wintered at Parker's Ferry every year until the end of the war. And there he began, once again, to work. The summers were passed in Edgartown, on Martha's Vineyard, Massachusetts. Soon after he first arrived at Parker's Ferry, he invited the Doubledays to dinner. His precious Annette was in France. How would Nora, the local substitute, cope? Could Mary, the coloured help, manage to serve a fancy dinner? No one need have worried. The meal was superb: onion soup; *truite au bleu*; duck *à l'orange*; a 'wondrous' salad (the story and vocabulary is again Garson Kanin's); and an almond soufflé. How was it achieved? 'No trouble at all,' Maugham told Kanin, 'unless you call trouble having the same meal eight nights running.'

He set much store by the places where he worked and preferred 'a salubrious climate'; both of his American homes suited him admirably. If he regretted France, he made no fuss, but his reading was often in French. *The Razor's Edge*, which he

The film of *The Moon and Sixpence*;
George Sanders as Charles Strickland.

began in the autumn of 1942, but for which many notes and plans had been made
earlier, is partly set in France and the cocotte, Suzanne Rouvier, is a portrait of a type
of Frenchwoman that Balzac painted in his lives of the courtesans and who incarnates
the amorous calculation and the self-reliant cheerfulness that Maugham found more
agreeable in women than the cloying dependence of the Anglo-Saxon. In the
autumn of 1942, *The Moon and Sixpence*, directed by Albert Lewin and starring
George Sanders, was premièred at the local movie house in Edgartown, which was
packed with celebrities. Maugham was gratified and, at the age of sixty-eight, made
the first of what were to be the very few public speeches he attempted during his
lifetime. As an Old Party, perhaps it mattered less to him what figure he cut,
provided that he cut a good one. He did. The film was very well done, though it now
seems dated. The director refrained from using Technicolor until the very end of the
picture, when Ashenden visits the hut where Strickland/Gauguin died and there sees
the masterpieces with which the walls have been covered.

Meanwhile, Gerald Haxton was drinking himself to death in Washington.
Maugham had already had a foretaste of what was coming when, at a party, Haxton
had more drinks than were good for him and proceeded to dive, fully clothed, into an
empty swimming-pool. He escaped with minor injuries but the novelist could hardly
fail to read the omens of the occasion. Haxton was over fifty; outrageousness can lose
its boyish charm when one passes the half-century. During 1943 Maugham worked
steadily on *The Razor's Edge*; his admiration for Larry Darrell's detachment – Larry's

Gene Tierney in the 1946 film of
The Razor's Edge.

charm was surely, in some measure, an idealization of Haxton's – came, in part, from his attempts to rise above the decay of the man whom he loved. There was no rift between them, but the old man was alone, far from Washington and powerless to save Gerald from himself.

The Razor's Edge was published in New York in April 1944 and in London in July. The war was not yet won, but there was no longer any question about who would win it. Although the novel was set firmly in the inter-war years, there were those who accused Maugham of trying to pander to an appetite for a new faith which might sustain those whom the conventional creeds and greeds of Western civilization had failed. Had not Christopher Isherwood already discovered the Vedanta and done much to popularize its message? The suggestion that Maugham had plunged into the Ganges as a result of some tardy calculation was plainly absurd; his interest in those who divested themselves of the lust and the avarice of the West was a constant feature of his fiction. Robert Calder's analysis of the unproduced play, *The Road Uphill*, written in 1924 and set in the Chicago of 1919, reveals a prototype scenario for the novel of 1944. Nor was the book in any sense out of character with its author. Just as it has increasingly been realized how right Nietzsche was in seeing that the Greeks' reverence for reason was the fruit of their sense of the power of the irrational, so those who accuse Maugham of hypocrisy would do well to accept that his veneration for the pure arose from a consciousness of his own impurity. What he had calculated, to a nicety, was the manner in which the story was told. It would be strange if he had

Maugham's popular venture into the realm of Oriental wisdom; Tyrone Power as Larry Darrell in *The Razor's Edge*.

not, but there is validity in the charge that, at his age (and with his wealth), he need not have sweetened the brew to quite such a degree. The confectioner in him even advises those who have no taste for Eastern philosophy to omit certain chapters, though he does say that had it not been for them, he would not have written the book. This supercilious deference to a public whose powers of attention he suspected to be so derisory is not only unflattering but unworthy. No great novelist need so distrust his own gifts; on the other hand, it might be said that there is no better device for getting a man to read something than to suggest that he may not be up to it.

Be that as it may, the public was once again given a service by his pen, not the full fruit or force of the man himself. He always kept something back. Like the prostitute he did not despise, he gave value for money, but it was for money; unlike Larry Darrell he always craved it. *The Razor's Edge* was an enormous success. It not only looked back with cultivated nostalgia on the Europe which was gone; it also reminded the victors, or those who would soon be victorious, of what a life without war might be like. It put in an early claim for the restoration of civilized concerns and pacific purposes. Before the war Maugham had believed that totalitarianism would eventually prevail, either from the Right or from the Left. He showed no inclination to put himself on the side of history; he hoped that the present phase would see him out. But nor did he rally to the Fascist side like so many of his rich friends. His brother was in Chamberlain's Cabinet; Willie thought the Lord Chancellor 'the most odious man I have ever met' and Churchill was a more frequent visitor to the Villa Mauresque. He had a place near by, at Roquebrune. As for the Left, Maugham's experience of Russia had forewarned him of the irresistible force of proletarian indignation and proletarian muscle. He did not see fit to join the Communist Party, as the richest artist in the world did; but he was not blind to the shape of things to come and, unlike H. G. Wells, his old neighbour, whom he met, disgusted and disillusioned in New York during the last years of the war, he had the strength to sketch a new personal morality which, if he could not live it himself, he believed might sustain and purify those who were sickened by the old ways but were uninclined to put their faith in principalities or powers. The success of *The Razor's Edge* may be attributed to the usual judicious mixture of drama and comedy, suspense and sex, but here also was a new, purging prescription written in a well-known specialist's hand. A new novel by Somerset Maugham, never mind its subject, was palatable evidence that the war had not changed everything. The old champion, like Joe Louis, was still there. Not everyone liked it, for all its measured freshness. Cyril Connolly wondered why:

It has puzzled me, considering the sheer delight that I and all my friends have received from this novel, that it has been so uncharitably received. Are we becoming incapable of recognising excellence when we see it?... I think prejudice is to blame – prejudice against any book which so perfectly captures the graces that have vanished, and against any writer who is so obviously not content with the banal routine of self-esteem and habit, graced by occasional orgies of nationalisation and herd celebrations, with which most of us ... fidget away our one-and-only lives.

The post-war voice of the Mandarin (with a dish of Socialist sour grapes before it) did not fail to speak a measure of the truth, but the weaknesses of *The Razor's Edge* have become more, rather than less, apparent. Despite this eulogy, Connolly, as editor of *Horizon*, later turned down a piece which Maugham wrote about the detective story. Even among his highbrow admirers, he was never regarded as pure gold. However that may be, Maugham had more to distress him at the end of 1944 than the captiousness of his critics. Gerald Haxton died in November of that year.

It is hard to estimate, from what has been written about him, exactly what Haxton's qualities were or what influence he had on Maugham. Most of those who write of him say plainly that he was no good. Beverley Nichols says that he stank. But the majority of those who speak ill of him might, to say the least, have relished the place in Maugham's life which he so unquestionably enjoyed. Nor is their own moral fineness always necessarily above suspicion. It may have seemed degrading that Maugham would come and fill a younger man's glass when Haxton crooked his little finger, but men have always performed services for those they love. Of Haxton's charm there is no question. He was described by Maugham as 'a useful companion' and so, all passion to one side, he undoubtedly was. It may be that he seduced Maugham, but mature men are seldom seduced for long into a pattern of sexual behaviour they find uncongenial. If he trapped Maugham, he also, on another reading, liberated him. He made him, to a degree, happy. Maugham was to say that he had never loved anyone who loved him. Haxton was doubtless amoral to a fault, but he gave Maugham a life – and the works of the twenties and thirties are there to prove it – which allowed him to do what he wanted. Haxton himself cannot always have been very happy; his years in Washington were an attempt to establish a separate identity for himself and Robin Maugham says that he had at last decided to make a life somewhere else than under Willie's shadow. The dog it was that died. Haxton contracted tuberculosis and all Willie's passionate and generous devotion were powerless to save him. Maugham returned, heartbroken, to Parker's Ferry. Robin Maugham, his brother Frederick's son, who had served in the Tank Corps during the North African campaign, went to stay with his uncle, who said of Haxton:

You'll never know how great a grief this has been to me. The best years of my life – those we spent wandering about the world – are inextricably connected with him. And in one way or another – however indirectly – all I've written during the last twenty years has something to do with him – if only that he typed my manuscripts for me.

It is not the most cordial of obituaries, but then W. Somerset Maugham was not an effusive man. He could not easily give himself and the expression of exaggerated sentiments was repugnant to him. He may have hated the type of the public-school Englishman; he was unable not to conform to it. It would be unimaginative to read in his guarded tributes to Haxton (they have the sound at times of an employer's reference) the measure of his appreciation. On the other hand, those who accuse Haxton of being Maugham's evil genius probably do him too much honour. The writer remains surprisingly proof against those who live with him. However cowed he may be socially, however served sexually, the writer's character remains obstinately selfish and self-expressive. He feeds on those he feeds and takes from them more than

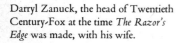
Darryl Zanuck, the head of Twentieth Century-Fox at the time *The Razor's Edge* was made, with his wife.

94

he gives. What matters most to him are the hours of solitude and what is produced during them. The most disturbing thing about Syrie was, according to Maugham, her appetite for scenes, especially late at night. It may be unromantic, but at a certain hour the diligent writer looks at his watch. Real life is all very well, but at nine in the morning he has fiction to serve. It is still the habit in Hollywood, where Maugham went in the summer of 1945, for dinner-parties to break up soon after ten; in the great days, stars had to be at the studio soon after six. Irregular behaviour is tolerated, but irregular hours simply will not do. Such is the life of the professional if he is to produce an *œuvre*, or even a movie.

Maugham was in California for the preparations for the inevitable film of *The Razor's Edge*. George Cukor was to direct, but the studio was not happy with the script. Maugham was not only not happy: he was so horrified by the version he read that he sat down in Cukor's house and in three months wrote a new script without charge; the book meant that much to him. Twentieth Century-Fox were as uneasy at such generosity as the delegation from Toulon had been when Maugham proposed that they site their guns *gratis* on Cap Ferrat. An *honorarium* was arranged; Maugham should have a painting instead of money. But what painting? A $15,000 painting. It came down to a Matisse snow scene or a particularly charming Pissarro, a view of Rouen harbour. After advice about investment values, he chose the Matisse. When he had completed the screenplay (in manuscript), Darryl Zanuck and Cukor pronounced themselves delighted. It then took another dozen drafts by Lamar Trotti before everyone was satisfied. Some years later, Maugham cashed the Matisse and acquired the Pissarro. Rouen was the home town of Gustave Flaubert.

Several of Maugham's stories were filmed (especially 'Rain', which has been done three times), but he was not at his best with film or with film people. Hollywood had

Back at the Villa after the war.

few comfortable memories. He had had a frigid encounter with René Clair in 1941 – Clair was later to say, cruelly, that Maugham knew nothing about France (on the shallow evidence of his short story 'Appearance and Reality') – and one may doubt whether his script for *The Razor's Edge* was necessarily as good as California politeness insisted.

At the end of 1945, Alan Searle, who had been Maugham's friend since the early thirties, became his secretary and companion. Here was a man no less worldly than Gerald Haxton, but of a different disposition. He was thoughtful and he was reliable. He was tactful with guests and with age. Maugham was lucky to have him, and he knew it. Together they went back to France.

The Villa Mauresque had not had a quiet war. It had been looted by the French, sacked by the Italians (when they invaded in May 1940), commandeered by the Germans (when they invaded in 1943) and then shelled by the British (when the Allies invaded in 1944). Mr Maugham's wine had been drunk, his garden sown with mines and his house damaged. But the Gauguin panels were still in their place. Most of the books and movable treasures had been hidden and whatever had been stolen was, for the most part, found and returned through the good offices of the Allied Control Commission. Places in the sun have a habit of recovering quickly, especially when a man has the means and resources, even in a period of shortages, to bribe the locals to put his house in order, smartly. This Maugham did. 'What a noble animal is man,' he wrote in *Then and Now*. 'With audacity, cunning and money there is practically nothing he cannot do.' And who shall blame him? He was seventy-two and he wanted to die in his own home, but not yet. Alan Searle's company gave him a new taste for life.

He resumed writing. Some war-horses function best in their stables. In 1947 normal service to his public was resumed with *Creatures of Circumstance*, a collection of stories. Heinemann's first run was of 50,000 copies. Maugham, like Goya, was not precocious, but he had staying power. The stories were largely from the past (the one that wasn't, 'The Unconquered', is a concocted tribute to the French, undefeated even in defeat) and they brought to a London still rationed, and having just come through the coldest winter for a century, a taste of the wide world of which wartime siege and post-war penury had deprived it. Alan Searle had once been a prison visitor, and readers of 'The Kite' and the other stories which feature Ned Preston may there find an affectionate picture of the companion of Maugham's old age.

Then and Now came out in 1946, though Laurence Brander affirms that it was actually written before the war. If so, one cannot but wonder whether Maugham did not at first decide not to publish it. It is the fruit of a lifelong admiration for the person and the clear thinking of Niccolò Machiavelli. Maugham had visited Florence during his vacations from St Thomas's, back in the early nineties, and now, with that taste for tying up ends which distinguished his notion of form, he dwelt, in his penultimate novel, on the genius of the Borgias and the brilliance of the man who wrote *The Prince* and *Mandragola*. Mr Brander suggests that the discussion of power and politics was prompted by the dominance of Hitler and Mussolini; they had, however, both been defeated before Maugham decided to publish. Perhaps the menace of Stalin and the strength of his apparatus of repression was a more immediate spur to the publication of *Then and Now* and also of *Catalina*, which was to be the last of Maugham's novels and dealt in its turn with the machinery of ideological totalitarianism as manifested in the Holy Inquisition. Thus in his old age Maugham again, wisely or not, followed the advice of Andrew Lang and wrote historical novels. Now it was less the inexperience of youth than the failing powers of old age that made him crutch his invention with historical fustian. There is a measure of wit

A scene from the Maugham film *Encore* (1951); 'The Kite' with Hermione Baddeley.

and of wisdom in both books, but it is often suffocated by turgidity. He, who had always been careful not to be dull, was now sometimes very dull indeed. However, it is rare that a great writer imitates Thomas Mann and produces a Felix Krull in his old age; if Maugham might have been wiser to stop sharply with *The Razor's Edge*, there is something touching, no less than tedious, in these last tributes to Italy and to Spain, always, after France, the two countries of his heart.

Then and Now provoked Edmund Wilson's famous attack upon its author, 'The Apotheosis of Mr Maugham'. Wilson had already launched a couple of sighting shots in 1941 when he heard of Maugham's encounter, in California, with Gerald Heard, Aldous Huxley and Christopher Isherwood, whose flirtations with Eastern mysticism did not chime with Wilson's political or critical temper. Now came the broadside:

It has happened to me from time to time to run into some person of taste who tells me that I ought to take Somerset Maugham seriously, yet I have never been able to convince myself that he was anything but second-rate. . . . His novel *Then and Now* – which I had sworn to explore to the end, if only to be able to say that I had read a book of Maugham's through – opposed to my progress, through all the first half, such thickets of unreadableness that there were moments when I thought I should never succeed. . . . The language is such a tissue of clichés that one's wonder is finally aroused at the writer's ability to assemble so many and at his unfailing inability to put anything in an individual way.

This article, in *The New Yorker*, did not fail to provoke Maugham's admirers. Whether they remarked that 'a tissue of clichés' was itself a cliché may be doubted, but they appealed to the surly Wilson to stay final sentence until he had read some of the short stories.

I made shift to dine on a dozen. They are readable – quite entertaining. . . . Mr Maugham writes best when his language is plainest. But these stories are magazine commodities . . . on about the same level as Sherlock Holmes; but Sherlock Holmes has more literary dignity because it is less pretentious. Mr Maugham makes play with more serious themes, but his work is full of bogus motivations that are needed to turn the monthly trick. He is for our day, I suppose, what Bulwer Lytton was for Dickens': a half-trashy novelist, who writes badly, but is patronized by half-serious readers, who do not care much about writing.

The apology was more damaging than the original salvo. One is reminded of those who accused Balzac of being a 'feuilletoniste prétentieux qui truffe son récit de considérations générales pour faire bien'.* Yet in Maugham's case there was force in the charge. 'Half-trashy' was perhaps as unkind as it was inelegant, but the comparison with Conan Doyle, who was also a writer with a medical training, did not lack sense. Wilson seems, indeed, to have felt that he had now granted too much and was quick to poison his gift.

What effect did this onslaught have on the old man? He always said that he did not read reviews. He subscribed to a cuttings service at one time but, because of his travels, there came an occasion when he did not see his notices until they were out of date. He then found that what was no longer fresh was no longer either enjoyable or

* [a pretentious hack who lards his narrative with sweeping remarks in order to make an impression.]

painful; it was simply dead. He ceased to read the critics. However, it is hard to believe that some indignant friend did not hurry to tell him of Wilson's malice. Maugham could console himself that Wilson had failed, signally, in each of the departments in which he himself had triumphed: theatre, novel, short story. Such consolations do not invalidate, though they may partly explain, the criticism. It must be admitted that Maugham, like the oysters to which Wilson was presumably comparing him, does not always taste the same. He can be a splendid and ironic guide to the world and then, when you come to him again, he has become a bland and verbosely facile *raconteur*. Who will deny that *Then and Now* displays him as a popular Man Of Letters in the most tiresome sense? Despite his advocates (often fellow writers, who know how difficult it is to seem effortless), Maugham never obtained critical favour at the highest levels. True, he was an inviting target, with his huge sales and his huge wealth, but a correct verdict is not set aside because of the mixed motives of the judge. He did not lack admirers and certainly, when it came to passing an afternoon, he was better company than those who depreciated him. Partly what was missing in the work was that wealth of metaphysical and symbolical allusion which renders criticism a man's work. He was too clear to be great. To a degree, also, one suspects that his anti-Christian bias, at times mellow but often heavily satirical, sorted ill with the traditions of English literature in which academics were, and often remain, immersed. He lacked Eliot's liturgical nostalgia and he could not rise to the apocalyptic heights of D. H. Lawrence in the mantle of an ithyphallic Jeremiah. Edmund Wilson's charge abides, however one may seek to turn it aside: Maugham never understood how artists use English. He lived a life in translation; he did it brilliantly, but that is what he did.

Having finished his fictional *œuvre*, he decided to turn critic himself, though in the amiable tradition of André Maurois rather than of Dr Leavis's open-necked Puritanism. A Philadelphia publisher, John C. Winston, prevailed upon him to choose, abridge and write introductions for *Ten Great Novels* for the general reader. Maugham had always held that the art of reading was the art of skipping and now undertook, boldly, to do the reader's skipping for him. It was an act of studied literary insolence. What serious critic could fail to be scandalized at a truncated version of *Le Rouge et le Noir* or of *Pride and Prejudice*? One ventures to think that some might not be so sorry to find *Tom Jones* a little shorter than Fielding made it or *David Copperfield* shorn of a few flourishes, but to put the scissors into *Le Père Goriot* or even *Anna Karenina* suggests the kind of cosmetic surgery which scars but does not beautify. It is not always an improvement to reduce giants to pocket size. Yet Maugham's remarks about the great masters of fiction are lucid, informative and sensible. They are not, luckily, meant to be normative, for the creative mind is forever finding new rules by breaking old ones, but they are invaluable to the novice and worthless only to the Master. (He saw, unerringly, the psychological flaw in the plot of *Le Rouge et le Noir*.) Maugham's surgery no doubt brought the books to the attention of many who would not otherwise have picked them up and if some of his remarks, especially on the subject of Proust, whom he did not include, are notorious in their impertinence, he showed a thorough love of the authors and of their works and, even in the case of Proust, a respect for genius which success had not qualified and age did not dim. When his introductions were later serialized in *The Sunday Times* (Ian Fleming,

whose James Bond was a descendant of Ashenden, negotiated the sale), the series was described, by the editor, as 'one of the most distinguished and successful serials ever to appear in these columns'. Maugham rewrote most of the biographies before they were printed in *The Sunday Times*. Perhaps the best refutation of Edmund Wilson's accusation of vulgar commercialism was that a man of almost eighty found the time and the will to make so thorough a revision.

He continued to travel, occupying himself with essays when he was at home at the Villa Mauresque. In 1949 he published *A Writer's Notebook*; now at last he spread his hand as a collector of fictional material, disclosing how the trick was turned and how skilful was his play of the cards which chance dealt him. Although the material published was, of course, a mere fraction of his working notes, there could be no clearer earnest of his intention to abandon the writing of stories and novels. This time there was no going back. In the *Notebook* he revealed that he had in fact planned to write one last novel. It was to have been set in Bermondsey (how keen he was on wheels that came full circle!) and wags might have called it, had it been written, *Son of Liza of Lambeth*, but his researches into post-1945 Bermondsey left him with the impression that the vitality of the working class had been stifled by the Welfare State. He found the people well housed and well shod, but the spark was gone. Perhaps it was his spark, for he no longer carried the little black bag and the judgment he passed was superficial. Had Mr Attlee's Government really expunged character or poverty from those who lived south of the river?

The influence of *A Writer's Notebook* was wide and salutary. It reminded writers that life, no less than ideas, could form the basis of literature. It was artfully edited and forms a pendant to *The Summing Up*; it too is somewhat judicial, but it is less formal and is studded with informative and suggestive detail.

Maugham's fame showed no sign of abating. When he travelled it was to enjoy not only the countries he had known but also the money he had accumulated in them; often royalties could not, owing to prevailing currency regulations, be exported. He was a best-seller throughout the world, from Spain where he went frequently, to Japan, to which he paid a visit in 1959; since his money did not come to him, he packed his bags (with SOMERSET MAUGHAM on them in quickly legible writing to avoid delay at terminals) and went to it. Once, in Spain, after a long trip during which he did not spare himself the luxuries to which his blocked royalties entitled him, he called for his bill at one of the best hotels only to be told that for Don Guillermo they could not possibly make any charge. In 1951 his collected stories were published under the well-merited title, *The World Over*. Few paths and few coasts had not seen his footprints, and his imprint.

In 1948 had come a new apotheosis, to cadge Edmund Wilson's sarcastic term; four of his short stories were made into a film, *Quartet*, and Maugham appeared personally to introduce each section. A replica of his study in the Villa Mauresque was constructed at Pinewood Studios, England. He performed his little pieces of rehearsed spontaneity with exemplary charm and lack of fuss. The presence of the Old Party on the set at first created an unwonted mood of formality, but this was broken during one of the pauses in shooting by a member of the crew who approached the Master and, with firm professional camaraderie, said to him, ''Ave a cuppa tea, Somerset.' Somerset had a cup of tea.

Scenes from *Quartet*; *right*, 'The Facts of
Life'; *below*, 'The Colonel's Lady';
opposite, Maugham himself as compere.

Quartet was a considerable success. Two more films followed, with the same format, *Trio* (Maugham bestirred himself to write one of the screenplays) and *Encore*. The face, no less than the works, of the old man became famous. A kind of courage, recognizable in a wry wisdom (he did not fail to present his most personable cynicism), attracted a new public to him. The Villa Mauresque became more than ever a sort of Delphic Oracle by correspondence. Hundreds of letters and manuscripts arrived for advice or comment. Visitors were rarer, but not rare. The old man who saw little to admire in his fellow creatures, who fed them neither philosophies nor dreams, was probably more eagerly solicited for his opinions than any contemporary writer. He gave blunt advice without fuss and without censoriousness. Replying to his correspondence was a duty he did not shirk. A gentleman could do no other, though he did sometimes wish that people would send stamps as well as photographs of themselves.

The success of his film appearances encouraged him to proceed to introduce television versions of his stories (a whole new market was beginning for him) and to record them on gramophone records. He desisted from this after a short time; it was tiring and it was also painful. While recording the section from *Of Human Bondage* concerning the death of Philip's mother, he broke down and could not continue. 'I shall never get over her death,' he had said; and he never did. So much for purging the pain of his youth through writing it out of his system.

However, he enjoyed his last share of the spotlight. One evening in London he was at a dinner-party with David Lean, the film director. He excused himself early on the grounds of tiredness. 'I must go home to bed.' He bent towards Lean as he left and said, 'I'm not really going to bed. I'm going up to P-Piccadilly. I want to see my n-name in l-lights.'

He made shift to surround his last years with a mellow, even benign air. He would be eighty in 1954. He founded a prize, the Somerset Maugham Award, to allow one young novelist each year to travel the world as he had done. (When asked for advice about what to do with a young man who wanted to write, he had always said, 'Give him a hundred and fifty a year for five years and tell him to go to the devil.') He regretted the insularity of the British intelligentsia and hoped to widen its horizons. One of the first winners of the Award was Kingsley Amis, whose *Lucky Jim* prompted an irritable Maugham to speak of the new generation of working-class upstarts as 'scum', an unfortunate outburst of narrowmindedness which was to blemish, slightly, the genial reputation which his unostentatious urbanity had procured. But first came the triumph of Maugham's eightieth birthday. He had done what Edward Driffield did, and the dividends of longevity came rolling in, as he had said they would. In 1952 he had been awarded a Doctorate by Oxford University; now he was made a Companion of Honour by the Queen. The Garrick Club gave a dinner in his honour. Only Dickens, Thackeray and Trollope had been honoured with the same formal homage. Maugham's father, Robert, had proposed Thackeray for membership of the Club. Of the evening itself, Garson Kanin reports that

the occasion was stately and moving, but . . . it began in a disquieting nerve-testing way. Maugham was introduced, took a standing ovation and, when the guests had resumed their seats, began his address. He spoke the customary salutations, paused for a moment and said, 'There are many . . . virtues in . . . growing old.' He paused, he

Opposite, The Old Party in contemplative mood at the Villa Mauresque.

swallowed, he wet his lips, he looked about. The pause stretched out, he looked dumbstruck. The pause became too long – far too long. He looked down, studying the table top. A terrible tremor of nervousness went through the room. Was he ill? Would he ever be able to get on with it? Finally he looked up and said, 'I'm just . . . trying . . . to think what they are!'

The house, as can be imagined, came down.

If only, in the light of the future, it had. The celebrations of his eightieth birthday were so full that they seemed, somehow, at once a consummation and an interment. The BBC produced five of his plays and dramatized five of his stories. *The Vagrant Mood*, the essays he published in 1952, had had a first run of 40,000 copies and was still selling. He was unquestionably at the top of his profession. A Cambridge undergraduate revue of the time bore witness:

> *Willie, Willie, Willie Somerset Maugham*
> *You're at the top of the literary form,*
> *You'll be going on fine,*
> *Till you're ninety-nine,*
> *Willie, Willie, Somerset Maugham.*

He went on living and he went on writing. Writer's cramp had obliged him to wear a *corset digital* but the habit was stronger than he was. One must not exaggerate the anticlimax of his last decade. In 1959, he published *Points of View*, the entirely palatable fruit of his ripest thoughts. He continued to find joy in travelling; it was his form of gregariousness. He could not stop. In the year of his eightieth birthday he visited both Italy and Spain as well as travelling back to England in June in order to go to the Palace for his Companion of Honour. He found amiable consolations for Britain in her decline:

It is true that as a nation we are sadly impoverished, but in compensation as individuals we are freer. We have rid ourselves of many stupid prejudices. Relations between the sexes are more unconstrained. We are less formal in our dress and far more comfortable. We are less class-conscious. We are less prudish. We are less arrogant.

A Rouault painting in Maugham's collection.

Impoverished Maugham himself was not. He was obsessed with the avoidance of tax. He worried about money. If he could not take it with him, he had no inclination to see it taken from him. Although he was generous with his old school and with young writers, his fortune became a source more of anxiety, even irritation, than of satisfaction. His pictures were enormously valuable, yet they seemed to hang about his neck no less than on his walls. Their future led him into wrangles with his daughter and eventually, fearful also of the danger of theft (the era of big art robberies was just beginning), he decided to sell the large part of them. The theatrical canvases by Zoffany and others were bequeathed to the National Theatre and meanwhile they substituted for the Monets and the Picassos which had graced his white walls. The Impressionists were to raise over £500,000 when they were auctioned at Sotheby's. Meanwhile life went on at the Villa Mauresque. The mornings were still consecrated to writing. In the afternoons and evenings there were visitors, but fewer than before;

David Garrick acting, by Zoffany

Marie Laurencin.

G. H. Barrable, *Songs from Italy*. 'When
I was 18 . . . the illustrated weeklies at
Christmas gave their readers a large
coloured reproduction. . . . I got one of
them, and as a modest decoration pinned
it up in my sitting-room' (*Purely for My
Pleasure*, 1962).

At the age of eighty-eight, Maugham legally adopted his secretary, Alan Searle.

there was conversation and bridge and, when Maugham was alone with Alan Searle, there were bonfires. Maugham, who had told so much of his life in so many ways, was determined that no 'publishing scoundrel' should make damaging disclosures about him after his death. He wished to be remembered by the works he elected to publish and by nothing else, unless it was the Maugham Award and the benefactions to the King's School. He burned letters and manuscripts. It was a source of pleasure to him. Alan Searle may have regretted the wanton destruction, but the papers were not his to protect or conceal. Was the old man still haunted by the fear of homosexual revelations? His life was bereft of the serene contemplation which Larry Darrell or the 'yogis' might have enjoyed; he was full of remorse and of spite. The burning of his correspondence and of many diaries seems almost like an assault on those who might be lucky enough to survive him and who could have found pleasure or profit in what he was not around to enjoy. Yet he was still capable of kindness and of generosity. A young and unpublished writer visited him in the autumn of 1954:

. . . I could boast neither mutual acquaintance nor personal achievement. He replied [to my letter] at once, remarking that although I had not dated my letter, he hoped that I was still on the Riviera; he nominated a day for me to come to tea. Alan Searle, the loyal companion of Maugham's old age, met me with the car in the little *place* of St-Jean-Cap-Ferrat and we drove up to the Villa Mauresque. We waited in the drawing room for the Master. I can see him now, coming through the doors from the hall where hung the great grey Picasso, a small man, surprisingly brisk, in dark flannels, tweed sports jacket and, I believe, a Paisley scarf at his throat. 'Here's Mr Maugham,' Alan Searle said, and he was holding out his hand. I was reminded – no

Opposite, a meeting with a fellow pupil, Charles Etheridge, at King's School, Canterbury, in 1958.

doubt because I knew of his medical past – of an eminent physician who has come to see how we are today. He cannot give you much time but while you are there, you can be sure of his undivided attention. 'Now we'll see about getting you some tea. Or perhaps he'd prefer a drink?' It was four-thirty. 'Tea, thank you,' I said. A minute later, a white-jacketed manservant brought tea and *petits fours* badged with cherry hearts. I took my tea with lemon, for some uneasy reason, and was flattered to discover that Maugham did the same. I imagined at the time that a rather bad musical comedy for which I had provided the book was going to be put on in London. (It was, later, but not so anyone noticed, luckily.) Maugham was good enough to seem impressed. It had taken him ten years to get anything presented in London. He had seen *The Boy Friend*, a skit on the twenties which was a great success at the time, when he was last in London. 'I didn't enjoy the joke as much as I should,' he said. 'I couldn't share it, you see, because I stopped going to musical comedies in the nineties of the last century.'

After tea, just as he was telling me that I should get a job, he started to light a cigarette. The match jumped from his fingers and fell into the crevice between the cushions of the sofa on which we were sitting. He was suddenly an old man, flapping at the buried ember, in a little panic of elderly nervousness. I felt a great pity and affection for him. Later he asked me how old I was. When I told him, he said, 'You've got plenty of time, plenty of time.'

It is to be hoped that the length of this excerpt will be excused. The young writer was the author of the present book. Other visitors painted a more lurid, perhaps less juvenile picture. The death of Syrie in 1955 occasioned, we are told, an unseemly glee, to the accompaniment of a little chant, 'Tra-la-la, no more alimony, tra-la-la.' There is no need to detail all the instances of unworthiness which have been so ably collated by Willie's friends and relations. No one can doubt that old age unlatched a tongue which, when he was fully in control of himself, might have been sharp and even cruel but was seldom simply vindictive or foul. Yet he could still be excellent company; most of those who hawk the stories of his senility juxtapose examples of a wit that continued to bear caustic fruit. He was capable also of a tart generosity. On one occasion in the fifties he came across the room, in the Hôtel de Paris in Monte Carlo, to speak to George Axelrod, the author of *The Seven Year Itch*. 'Mr Axelrod,' he said, 'I am told that you are an extremely talented young man and all I can say is, thank G-God I'm too old to g-give a shit.' Such was the flattery of a nineties dandy who knew the business. He remained spry and, in a word which Beverley Nichols elected to find disparaging, spruce. He swam (and dived) regularly. He played bridge in good company. When he came to London, Kenneth Konstam and Guy Ramsey arranged games for him at Crockford's. He continued to write essays, joining the critical ranks with the resigned amusement of a parliamentarian promoted at last to an impotent Upper Chamber, and he continued to progress, like an old king, through the provinces of his literary empire. In 1957 he went back to Heidelberg, with its blushing castle still looking down on the old town; in 1958, on his annual visit to London, he was able to see and hear (through a hearing aid) an opera, based on *The Moon and Sixpence*, with music by John Gardner, produced at Sadler's Wells; in 1959 he made his last visit to the Far East. When he first published his stories about Malaya, indignant Colonials heaped anathemas on him. How could 'The Letter' ever be forgiven? But now old grievances had faded. He was received everywhere with honour. In Japan, 40,000 people attended a ten-day exhibition of his works.

Maugham at his favourite sport; a bridge-party arranged in his honour at Crockford's Club, London, in November 1953.

Even in the seventies Gore Vidal could regret the bad taste of the Japanese in still buying the old man's work in best-selling quantities. (Vidal's evangelical homosexuality marks the change in literary manners since, in the words of the singer Lou Reed, homosexuality came out of the closet and into the streets.)

On the way home from Japan, there were visits to Vietnam, to Cambodia, to Thailand and to Burma. Few of the world's stones had been left unturned in the service of 'the monthly trick', for these were all old stamping-grounds. It is hardly surprising that a man of eighty-six found the journey tiring. It was probably on his return that he began that series of injections at the Niehans' Clinic in Switzerland which, in the opinion of one well disposed towards him, 'gave his body a vigour that at that age his mind could not support'. On the other hand, senility's ungracious querulousness is not uncommon even among those who cannot afford expensive punctures. Be that as it may, the last years were certainly blemished by the vindictive paranoia which culminated in the publication, in 1962, of *Looking Back*. This memoir, which contained a good deal of rehashed material, was notorious above all for its caddish attack on Syrie. To revile his dead wife, the mother of his living daughter, in so coarse a fashion, accusing her of being a thief, an adulteress and a social climber, was inexcusable. Old friends broke with him; Oliver Messel wrote a dignified and credible defence of Syrie:

It seems impossible to understand what Mr Somerset Maugham hopes to achieve by writing in such a tasteless way about his dead wife, and what appears equally ignoble is the fact that it is his only child who must be hurt most by the pointless and spiteful picture he has chosen to present of a woman not alive to defend herself. As one of Syrie Maugham's many devoted friends for over 25 years, I would like to be allowed to say how astonishingly different was my own impression of this very remarkable and delightful woman. Far from being, as Maugham smugly attempts to portray her, a pleasure-seeking woman without resources, Syrie was one of the most resourceful intuitively brilliant women that I have been fortunate enough to meet. Her own creative flair in decoration influenced the whole trend of taste throughout the thirties, both in England and in America. I was still a student at the Slade when I first met Syrie. She inspired and helped me as she did so many young people on the brink of a career. She had dynamic energy and a stimulating mind. I can think of no one who was more fun to be with or who had more understanding and tenderness on occasions when one needed a friend most.

Catherine the Great; a bust by Shubin.

Her friends subscribed to a memorial to her, a bust of Catherine the Great by Fedor Shubin. It was presented to the Victoria and Albert Museum in 1964.

Although *Looking Back* was published in the U.S. as well as in Great Britain, it was rumoured that Lord Beaverbrook was the evil genius who incited Willie to such charmless frankness, frankness in all things save the old obsession, homosexuality. Beaverbrook is one of those to whom any evil design may plausibly be imputed, and it may well be that in offering £100,000 for the serial rights he screwed Maugham up to the unsticking point, but Beaverbrook was as shrewd a publisher as he was a mischief-maker and it was likely that acumen as much as malice led him to make the offer. For it cannot be denied that the disgraceful document made, and makes, excellent reading. There may indeed be fantasy mixed with the facts (no one denies that some details are plain wrong), but then Maugham's whole creative life – and he had been writing for seventy years – was just such an artful mixture. The denigration of Syrie and the sheer immodesty with which it was achieved lacks scruple as well as dignity. But Maugham had always said that to declare oneself fully would be to reveal a monster of depravity. Ironic detachment and a sense of grievance are two sides of a coin which, had he been wiser, Maugham might have done well not to spin in public. He probably regretted the scandal and the fuss, for he never returned to London and he forbade publication of *Looking Back* in volume form. There may be something to be said for not trying to get everything out of one's system. His last volume, *Purely for My Pleasure*, was published in the same year, 1962; it consisted largely of plates of his famous pictures. Works by Renoir, Bonnard, Matisse, Léger, Rouault, Picasso, Vuillard, Monet and Laurencin were among them. The text was secondary; the book was hardly more than a catalogue for the great sale which took place in the same year. Yet – and how often with Maugham a judgment must be

Somerset Maugham with his novelist nephew, Robin.

qualified! – the book was testimony to a lifetime devoted, in its fashion, to art, and it was proof that Maugham had valued the painter's art more than any other. He had found beauty and consolation and inspiration there; contemplation, wordlessness even, had long had its hold on him. In *Looking Back* there is a touching, perhaps pathetic, perhaps redeeming moment when, in Venice in 1958, he tells of a painting of Christ by Paolo Veronese which, he declared solemnly, turned and looked at him. 'Jesus Christ', he told Robin Maugham, 'could cope with all the miseries I have had to contend with in life. But then Jesus Christ had advantages I don't possess.' Christianity did not always, after all, wear the face of the vicar of Whitstable.

Maugham grew older and older. He rambled. He forgot himself. He was an embarrassment to his friends. He wept tears of self-pity at his sufferings and of remorse at his wickednesses. But if he had hurt or shocked many of those closest to him, he had been a comfort and a consolation to millions who knew him only by the trademark which promised to deliver the goods, and usually did. At last, in the winter of 1965 he was taken gravely ill at the Villa Mauresque and transported to the British–American Hospital in Nice. He had always wanted to die at the Villa. He

The repository of Maugham's ashes at King's School.

Opposite, a view of Canterbury Cathedral.

was almost ninety-two years old when Alan Searle, knowing that there was nothing further to be done, had him moved once more to Saint-Jean-Cap-Ferrat where, on 16 December 1965, he died. He was cremated and the ashes were flown home to England and buried at King's School, Canterbury, where he had been utterly wretched and where his benefactions surrounded him like coals of fire.

Anthony Curtis's centenary study, *The Pattern of Maugham,* concludes with the mandatory estimate of the writer's abiding worth. Its praise of Maugham's narrative skill verges on the whimsical but a valid point is made: although a writer can expect to be judged by his best work, it is a hard thing to do in Maugham's case because 'the essential Maugham is Maugham'. How does one carve the long unity of his *œuvre*? He is greater than the sum of his parts, and it is probably just as well. When all is said and done, however, the paradox remains: he is not a great writer and yet he is on the side of greatness. He was not a charitable man and yet he advocated no bullying creed. He found it hard to find or give love, but longed for it all his life. He was a commercial writer, but he knew that great literature is beyond price. He claimed to be only a story-teller, but craved a Truth above fictions. He boasted that he had no illusions about his fellow men but, as Noël Coward tellingly observed, he had just one illusion about them and that was that they were no good. On the other hand, how wrong was he? He lived through the era of Imperialism and Colonialism and he witnessed the most murderous wars in history; in his lifetime took place cruelties beyond the dreams of Torquemada and mass murder on a scale no Borgia ever envisaged. Perhaps he was embittered only by the chance that he said had ruled his life and which robbed him of his mother and father at an early age and sent him to live among bigots and Philistines, but it cannot really be argued that the world was ill-used by his pen. Whatever the merits of Maugham's work in strict eyes, on their dangerous voyage through eternity, human beings can at least sit on deck and read his stories. They will not necessarily arrive at a happier destination, but it will entertain them on the way. And if they can find better things to do? The author would say that they should please themselves.

CHRONOLOGY

1874 25 January: William Somerset Maugham born at the British Embassy in Paris.

1882 Death of his mother in childbed.

1884 Death of his father. Maugham is sent to live with his uncle in Whitstable, Kent, and attends junior annexe of the King's School, Canterbury.

1890 While convalescing on the Riviera from a lung infection, Maugham discovers French literature.

1891 After leaving the King's School, Maugham spends nine months in Heidelberg where he attends lectures on philosophy and literature.

1892 Enrols as a medical student at St Thomas's Hospital, London.

1895 Works for three weeks as an obstetric clerk in the slums of Lambeth.

1897 Publication of *Liza of Lambeth* by Fisher Unwin. Maugham turns down the offer of an assistantship at St Thomas's and decides on a literary career.

1898–1903 Maugham travels in Spain and Italy. His novels and stories meet with little success.

1903 Maugham's first play, *A Man of Honour*, is performed by the Stage Society. He becomes co-editor of *The Venture* with Laurence Housman, but settles in Paris after its failure.

1907 Successful première of *Lady Frederick* at the Royal Court Theatre. Within a year Maugham has four plays running in the West End.

1913 Maugham begins his liaison with Syrie Wellcome.

1914–15 After serving with the Ambulance Unit in France, Maugham is recruited into Military Intelligence and takes up a posting in Geneva.

1915 August: Publication of *Of Human Bondage*, begun in 1911.

1916 Journey to the South Seas with Gerald Haxton. Discovery of Gauguin panels. On his return Maugham marries Syrie.

1917 Maugham is sent to St Petersburg by British Intelligence in an attempt to bolster the Provisional Government of Kerensky. On his return from Russia he enters Banchory Sanitorium.

1919 Publication of *The Moon and Sixpence*. Second visit to the South Seas. Maugham begins a decade of travelling in the Far East, the United States, Europe and North

Africa. His short stories, plays, novels and travel-sketches bring him increased fame and popularity.

1927 Maugham and Syrie divorce.

1928 Maugham buys the Villa Mauresque on Cap Ferrat. Publication of *Ashenden*.

1930 Publication of *Cakes and Ale*. Maugham's literary output continues throughout the thirties, although he retires from the theatre in 1933.

1936 Visit to the West Indies.

1938 Visit to India. A second visit, planned for the following year, is prevented by the outbreak of war.

1940 Denounced personally by Goebbels, Maugham flees from Nice. In October he leaves London for the United States where he remains for the duration of the war, wintering at Parker's Ferry, South Carolina, and spending the summers at Edgartown, Martha's Vineyard.

1942 Film première of *The Moon and Sixpence* at Edgartown.

1944 Publication of *The Razor's Edge*. Death of Gerald Haxton.

1945 Maugham works in Hollywood on the film-script of *The Razor's Edge*. Alan Searle becomes his secretary and companion.

1946 Return to the Villa Mauresque. Foundation of the Somerset Maugham Award.

1948 Maugham's successful presentation of a film version of four of his short stories, *Quartet*, is followed by *Trio* (1950) and *Encore* (1951).

1950 Introduces television versions of his stories.

1952 Awarded Doctorate by Oxford University.

1954 At the age of eighty Maugham is given a dinner of honour at the Garrick Club and becomes a Companion of Honour. The BBC produces five of his plays and dramatizes five of his stories.

1955 Death of Syrie.

1959 Last visit to the Far East.

1962 Publication of *Looking Back* containing notorious attack on Syrie.

1965 Taken gravely ill at the Villa Mauresque, Maugham is transported to the British-American Hospital in Nice. He is brought back to Cap Ferrat where he dies on 16 December.

BIBLIOGRAPHY

There is no official, or indeed authoritative, biography of Somerset Maugham. He did not want there to be one and he destroyed many papers which might have been germane to such a work. I cite here books which I have found useful or worthy of note. Others will be found in Raymond Toole Stott's invaluable bibliography.

Ronald F. Barnes *The Dramatic Comedy of W. Somerset Maugham* (1968)

Fred Bason 'Mr Somerset Maugham', in *The Saturday Book* (1945)

—*Diary* (1950)

Arnold Bennett *Journals* (1932/3)

Laurence Brander *Somerset Maugham, a Guide* (1963)

John Brophy *Somerset Maugham* (1952)

Robert L. Calder *W. Somerset Maugham and the Quest For Freedom* (1972)

Cyril Connolly *Enemies of Promise* (1938)

—*The Condemned Playground* (1946)

R. A. Cordell *William Somerset Maugham* (1961)

Noël Coward *A Song at Twilight* (play) (1967)

Aleister Crowley *The Confessions of Aleister Crowley* (1969)

Anthony Curtis *The Pattern of Maugham* (1974)

Peter Daubeny *My World of Theatre* (1971)

Rupert Hart-Davis *Hugh Walpole* (1952)

Robert Hichens *Autobiography* (1947)

K. W. Jonas *The Gentleman from Cap Ferrat* (1956)

Garson Kanin *Remembering Mr Maugham* (1966)

Desmond MacCarthy *W. Somerset Maugham, 'The English Maupassant'* (1934)

Louis Marlow *Seven Friends* (1953)

Robin Maugham *Somerset and All the Maughams* (1966)

—*Escape from the Shadows* (1972)

Beverley Nichols *A Case of Human Bondage* (1966)

Harold Nicolson *Diaries and Letters* (1966)

Karl G. Pfeiffer *Somerset Maugham, A Candid Portrait* (1959)

Victor Purcell *The Memoirs of a Malayan Official* (1965)

A. Riposte (Elinor Mordaunt) *Gin and Bitters* (1931)

Cecil Roberts *Sunshine and Shadow* (1972)

J. C. Trewin *The Theatre Since 1900* (1951)

Edmund Wilson *Classics and Commercials* ('The apotheosis of Somerset Maugham') (1950)

Godfrey Winn *The Infirm Glory* (1967)

SOMERSET MAUGHAM'S WRITINGS

The following list is less than exhaustive, but I have included both works it would be self-important to omit and those on which the author's reputation more properly depends.

NOVELS AND SHORT STORIES:
Liza of Lambeth (1897); *Mrs Craddock* (1902); *Of Human Bondage* (1915); *The Moon and Sixpence* (1919); *The Trem-*

bling of a Leaf (1921); *The Painted Veil* (1925); *The Casuarina Tree* (1926); *Ashenden* (1928); *Cakes and Ale* (1930); *First Person Singular* (1931); *The Narrow Corner* (1932); *Ah King* (1933); *Cosmopolitans* (1936); *Theatre* (1937); *Christmas Holiday* (1939); *The Mixture as Before* (1940); *The Razor's Edge* (1944); *Then and Now* (1946); *Creatures of Circumstance* (1947); *Catalina* (1948).

TRAVEL, ESSAYS AND BELLES LETTRES:
On a Chinese Screen (1922); *Don Fernando* (1935); *The Summing Up* (1938); *A Writer's Notebook* (1949); *The Vagrant Mood* (1952); *Points of View* (1958).

PLAYS:
The plays have been collected in three volumes, with introductions by the author, published by William Heinemann, who published all Maugham's work from *Mrs Craddock* onwards. The plays and the collected short stories have also been published by Penguin, and in other paperback editions.

LIST OF ILLUSTRATIONS

75 ETHELWYN SYLVIA JONES; painting by Gerald Kelly. *Courtesy of Lady Kelly*

76 CYRIL CONNOLLY; drawing by Augustus John, 1945. Private Collection

JACKET FOR *First Person Singular* by W. Somerset Maugham, 1931. *Courtesy of Bertram Rota Ltd*

77 STILL FROM J. ARTHUR RANK FILM *Quartet*, 1948. *Courtesy of the Rank Organisation*

81 CONVENT OF ST TERESA OF AVILA, SEVILLE

82 W. SOMERSET MAUGHAM AND FRIENDS AT SALZBURG, *c.* 1935. *Mansell Collection*

83 P. & O. POSTER. *Courtesy P. & O. Photographic Library*

84 FREDERICK HERBERT, FIRST LORD MAUGHAM in Lord Chancellor's robes; portrait by Gerald Kelly, 1939. Trinity Hall, Cambridge. *Photo courtesy of Lord Maugham*

85 HAROLD NICOLSON AND VICTORIA SACKVILLE-WEST, 1932. *Courtesy of N. Nicolson*

86 GARSON KANIN AND RUTH GORDON. *Photo Graphic House, New York*

87 FRENCH REFUGEES FROM GERMAN ADVANCE, 1940. *Imperial War Museum, London*

88 W. SOMERSET MAUGHAM AT WORK, Dorchester Hotel, London, 1940. *Radio Times Hulton Picture Library*

90 GEORGE SANDERS in the film *The Moon and Sixpence*, directed by Albert Lewin, 1942. *National Film Archive*

91 GENE TIERNEY in the film *The Razor's Edge*, 1946. Twentieth Century-Fox. *National Film Archive*

92 TYRONE POWER in the film *The Razor's Edge*, 1946. Twentieth Century-Fox. *National Film Archive*

94 VIRGINIA AND DARRYL ZANUCK. *Radio Times Hulton Picture Library*

95 A VIEW OF ROUEN; painting by Camille Pissarro, 1896. *Courtesy of Sotheby's, London*

96 W. SOMERSET MAUGHAM in a still from *Encore*, 1951. *Courtesy of the Rank Organisation*

97 MERVYN JOHNS, HERMIONE BADDELEY AND GEORGE COLE in the film *Quartet*, 1948. *Courtesy of the Rank Organisation*

100 W. SOMERSET MAUGHAM; painting by Graham Sutherland, 1949. *Tate Gallery*

102 STILL FROM *Quartet*, 1948. *Courtesy of the Rank Organisation*

STILL FROM *Quartet*, 1948. *Courtesy of the Rank Organisation*

103 W. SOMERSET MAUGHAM in a still from *Quartet*, 1948. *Courtesy of the Rank Organisation*

105 W. SOMERSET MAUGHAM in a still from *Encore*, 1951. *Courtesy of the Rank Organisation*

106 CRUCIFIXION; painting by Georges Rouault, 1939. *Courtesy of Sotheby's, London*

107 D. GARRICK AS JAFFIER in Otway's *Venice Preserv'd*; painting by J. Zoffany (1733–1810). *Photo: Victoria and Albert Museum, Crown Copyright*

THREE GIRLS IN A BOAT; painting by Marie Laurencin, 1926. *Courtesy of Sotheby's, London*

SONGS FROM ITALY; print after G. H. Barrable, *c.* 1890

108 W. SOMERSET MAUGHAM, aged eighty-eight, with Alan Searle. *Camera Press*

109 THE MEETING OF W. SOMERSET MAUGHAM WITH FELLOW PUPIL CHARLES ETHERIDGE at King's School, Canterbury, 1958. *Courtesy of the King's School, Canterbury*

111 W. SOMERSET MAUGHAM, aged seventy-nine, at bridge-party, Crockford's, London. *Radio Times Hulton Picture Library*

112 CATHERINE THE GREAT by F. Shubin, 1771. *Victoria and Albert Museum, Crown Copyright*

113 ROBIN MAUGHAM WITH W. SOMERSET MAUGHAM. *Courtesy of Lord Maugham*

114 THE ASHES OF W. SOMERSET MAUGHAM, buried 22 December 1965. *Photo Kentish Gazette*

115 CANTERBURY CATHEDRAL. *Courtesy of the King's School, Canterbury*

116 W. SOMERSET MAUGHAM in a
–17 still from *Encore*, 1951. *Courtesy of the Rank Organisation*